AMERICA
from the Heart
QUILTERS REMEMBER SEPTEMBER 11, 2001

Curated by Karey Bresenhan

C&T PUBLISHING

A Message from the Publisher:
This book came about after a group of staff members from C&T viewed the moving exhibit during Quilt Market in October 2001. Along with the rest of the nation and the world, we were shocked and saddened by the terrorist attacks on September 11, 2001. We looked for appropriate ways to commemorate the victims and contribute to relief efforts. We decided on the spot to create a catalog of these quilts so that quilters around the world could share in this remarkable exhibit. This project would not have been possible without the untiring efforts of Karey Bresenhan, Nancy O'Bryant of Quilts, Inc. and Amy Marson, Kristen Yenche, and Tim Manibusan of C&T Publishing. C&T Publishing and Quilts, Inc. are proud to donate all profits from the sales of *America from the Heart,* to the Families of Freedom Scholarship Fund.

C&T Publishing would like to thank Regent Publishing Services for donating a portion of the printing to benefit the Families of Freedom Scholarship Foundation.

© 2002, C&T Publishing

Publisher: Todd Hensley

Editors: Amy Marson, Jan Grigsby

Design Director/Book Designer/Cover Designer: Kristen Yenche

Production Assistant: Timothy Manibusan

Proofreaders: Stacy Chamness, Carol Barrett

Photography: Jim Lincoln, Jim Lincoln Photography

Published by C&T Publishing, Inc., P.O. Box 1456, Lafayette, California 94549

Front cover: *Spirits Rising* by Betsy Shannon

Back cover: *Quilt of Compassion* by Laura Fogg and Betty Lacy, *Sweet Land of Liberty* by Miri Cook

Editor's note: In order to display the quilt images as large as possible the artist's statements were edited. The miscellaneous quotes are excerpts from the memory book made by Maxine Farkas for Fall '01 Quilt Festival. Due to legal issues the following exhibited quilts have been omitted from this book; *Long May She Wave* by Barbara W. Barber, *New York Firemen* by Dorthy Theall, *9/11* by Ellen Rosintoski, *Those Who Answered the Call* by Bonnie Peterson, *Tears Over U.S.* by Leslie Blair Gallagher, *Tower II: Destruction of the World Trade Center* by Patricia Montgomery, *Tolerance* by Mei-Ling St. Leger.

Photographs and logos reprinted by permission: page 89, Rick Flores/*The Journal News*/Corbis Sygma; page 69, Debbie and Michael Markowitz, page 52, *The New York Times;* page 24, Daniel Stonek, Peter Morgan/Reuters; page 92, Annette M. Lellis, NY Ad Council page 65, Ted Harriss. Stock photography used throughout the book courtesy of Photospin.com

Poem reprinted by permission: page 126, Peter Mitchell McCulloch

Library of Congress Cataloging-in-Publication Data
America from the heart : quilters remember September 11, 2001 / curated by Karey Bresenhan.
    p. cm.
Includes index.
ISBN 1-57120-145-9 (paper trade)
    1. Quilts--United States--History--20th century--Catalogs. 2. September 11 Terrorist Attacks, 2001--Art and the terrorist attacks--Catalogs. I. Bresenhan, Karey
    NK9112 .A52 2002
        746.46'09'05110747641411--dc21
                                            2002000837

Printed in China

10 9 8 7 6 5 4 3 2 1

Foreword

On September 11, when the towers collapsed, the Pentagon burst into flame, and the plane went down in Pennsylvania, the world as we knew it changed forever. No longer were Americans blessed with safety, isolated between two huge oceans. No longer was there "one safe place" that even people in other countries had come to depend on.

The quilters of America reacted no differently than the rest of their fellow countrymen. They were stunned, horrified, shocked, disbelieving of what their own eyes showed them, consumed by grief, baffled, and finally angry. Like everyone else, they were paralyzed in front of their televisions, watching through tears as the grim events unfolded and the death toll mounted. They were struck to the heart when the Twin Towers fell, killing not only thousands of office workers but also hundreds of rescue workers, those brave men and women who had, without thought for themselves, rushed into the stricken buildings in a doomed effort to save anyone they could. And after the tears, when they felt they could cry no more, the quilters turned to their art to try to make sense of the senseless tragedy that had hit our country. Quilters in other countries, too, felt that same compulsion to work out their anger and grief in quilts that conveyed the statement we heard over and over: "Today, we, too, are Americans. We stand with you and we grieve with you."

Because I participate in an online discussion group, QuiltArt, I knew how grief-stricken and frustrated many of the quilt artists were. Reading how they were trying to make quilts to work through their sorrow and anger, I realized that many quilters everywhere were probably facing the same challenge. So shortly after the tragedies, I announced on QuiltArt, on our own website, and on other websites that we would create a spontaneous exhibit—*AMERICA: From the Heart*—to be seen at the International Quilt Market and International Quilt Festival in Houston, then only six weeks away. Although the show was sold out, and we already had more than 35 special quilt exhibits, which left us absolutely no room to add another one, I was determined that these quilts had to be seen. So I told the quilters: you make them, we'll hang them. *We'll show every quilt that's submitted.* No rules, no jurying, just quilts from the heart. The only restrictions were that we would show no quilts that conveyed messages of hate, and we reserved the right to remove a quilt if it created undue distress.

I expected perhaps fifty quilts. Instead, we received almost 300! And that brought another last-minute challenge—where in an already full show could we possibly make room to show

300 quilts? Our solution was to create "a wall of images and messages," resembling those heartbreaking walls of pictures of the missing that sprang up daily in New York City. Our wall ran right across the middle of the show, in the center of the wide "Main Street" aisle, right under the huge American flag.

The quilts came in the day before we hung the show, and a few continued to come in, caught up in the vagaries of mail delivery, even during the show. We hung every quilt.

The resulting exhibit was unforgettable, moving, heartbreaking, and inspiring. The quiltmakers ranged from world-class quilt artists to women creating their first quilt, to 5th graders. They were not only American but also Canadian, Israeli, and Japanese. They sent quilts from Australia, New Zealand, Scotland, Spain, and the United Arab Emirates.

To watch the thousands of visitors to the International Quilt Festival who studied the exhibit was to see pure emotion on unembarrassed display: tears rolling silently down cheeks, little children being lifted up to see certain details of a quilt their parents deemed important for them to remember, a hand seeking out the human contact of another hand to hold. But inevitably, the tears would cease, the back would straighten, the chin would go up, and a look of resolute determination would overshadow the sorrow.

We felt it was important to share these quilts with people who were unable to visit the show. C&T Publishing and Quilts Inc., have collaborated to bring you this moving catalog in which all profits will be donated to the Families of Freedom Scholarship fund, the same fund that was selected as the beneficiary of the $25,000 raised in the Silent Auction of approximately 100 of the AMERICA quilts.

That these quilts, made so quickly in a catharsis of grief and anger, could have such an effect on the viewers of the exhibit is a testimony to the power of art to touch people's hearts.

—Karey PattersonBresenhan

Director, International Quilt Market and International Quilt Festival Houston, Texas

The World Expresses its Sorrow, Shock & Vulnerability

Thank you to all the artists for helping us in our shared grief.

RESOLVE, **34" x 22"**, **Erlene Irwin**, Lexington, VA USA

As I sat watching the events of September 11, 200I, this image kept coming to mind. I knew I needed to make a quilt, but who would want to look at such a painful thing? Finally, when I could stand it no longer, I started to work. It was many days later when I realized the message of my quilt. Part of the American Spirit has been the resolve to do what is needed, no matter the price, pain, or insurmountable odds. Seeing firefighters, police, emergency personnel, volunteers, and anyone available do remarkable things during this awful time, reminded me that there is some beauty in all things. The beauty of the American Spirit was shining through. I dedicate my work to this spirit.

OUR WORLD IS CHANGED

22" x 36" Jean Dunn
Marina, CA USA

This image will be with me forever.

Always Remember! 9-11

INNOCENTS LOST

40½" x 60" Jan Brashears
Cumming, GA USA

The disaster of 9-11-01 was devastating to our nation in ways no other event has been. The twin buildings are shown from the beginning of the morning through later in the day. Raw edges are everywhere to emphasize the raw nerves and energy that coursed with each revelation. The colors of red and black are used heavily to depict the physical damage to people and property. In doing the piece, I used actual headlines from newspapers to emphasize the scope of the desolation. The title refers to the many innocent people who died or were injured to accomplish the work of the terrorists. Until the completion of the quilt, I had images in my head of the piece and was driven to do the work. Now that Innocents Lost is finished, my catharsis is complete, my head is clear. My heart is still sad.

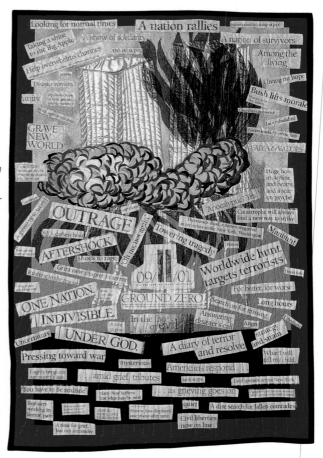

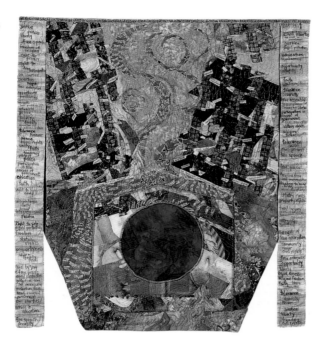

UNTITLED (THERE ARE NO WORDS)

28½" x 31½" Laura Cater-Woods
Billings, MT USA

On the morning of September 11, 2001, a friend telephoned, "Turn on the television." Immediate thoughts were for families and friends: where is everyone, are they okay, is everyone accounted for? But of course, not everyone is okay, not everyone is accounted for. Some are simply gone. All the families affected. All the lives, interrupted. For the past few months I had been working on pieces for a solo exhibit next spring. Now I found myself unable to work in my studio… however, the America: From the Heart exhibit gave me a framework to wrap my thoughts and emotions around. The piece that had been in progress on the wall was cut up and interwoven with raw cloth. The construction methods became a visual metaphor for me. Some edges are raw and frayed, batting is left exposed, threads are hanging…The shield shape of the center panel was unexpected. The side panels are the "words to live by," the rights and freedoms we take for granted. I see these two panels as prayer flags.

The words across the top of the piece are reminders that our recent experience is one that many other cities and nations have been living with for too long.

As a nation we are experiencing for the first time what huge numbers of people on the planet have been living with for decades. I think we must ask ourselves if we are living our values, if we are conducting our business in accordance with the rights we hold dear.

RIVERS OF WATER

20½" x 23½" Helen Simon
Lake Charles, LA USA

Expressing my extreme anguish at our disregard of God's law, my quilt is a plea of hope, created to inspire us to return to God's direction for our lives.

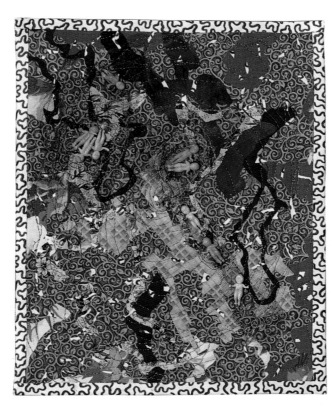

THE FINAL JUMP

14" x 11" Linda Sorkin Eisenberg
Chicago, IL USA

Not unlike the world, September 11th had a major impact on me. I was able to work out some of my sadness and anger as I began to create this piece. It became extremely cathartic and intense.

While I was working I continually visualized the craziness, as the flames erupted in the towers. I saw people and their horror, fear and anxiety take over as they were mindfully trying to make the best decisions possible, for several days that was all that I thought about.

During my creation of The Final Jump, *I began my process. The question I kept asking myself was "what I would have done in their shoes?" It became very clear to me that I would join hands with those that decided to jump, and we would become a human chain. By doing that I knew that I would not feel as alone and that this would give me comfort.*

To all of you who poured your hearts out with such beautiful results. Thank you!

TOO MANY

12" x 12" Cheryl Kagen
West Seneca, NY USA

9/11/01: I am at work, a co-worker comes in and asks if we have heard. We all gather around the TV in the hall that only gets one channel (and that one very poorly), the second tower gets hit, then comes the report that the Pentagon fire was caused by a third plane. I am a Jewish woman, never denying my faith, but rarely participating in public observations. My overwhelming urge is to fall to my knees and pray—the rage and fear build as I hold myself back—I've never felt such feelings in my life. My co-workers stand in disbelief, some crying...the details keep coming in and coming in—and just when you think you've heard the worst, you HAVEN'T.

This quilt: Over the last few weeks, the men and women and children who were murdered have been described in round numbers—every once in a while we get a specific name or a specific number. Twenty years ago I took a trip to Israel—my strongest memory of that trip was being at the Yad Vashem memorial—a large room where you walk above a floor covered in six million one-inch tiles, each representing one Jewish man, woman, or child killed in the Holocaust. Six million one-inch tiles take up an amazing amount of space! I make this very small piece with the same idea in mind—EACH person murdered was an individual who was part of a group that knew them, loved them, and now miss them terribly...

MOUNTAIN OF SORROW

60" x 50" Jill Havrilla Caban
Long Valley, NJ USA

Creating this quilt helped me to lessen the weight on my heart from the mountain of sorrow left behind where the Twin Towers of the World Trade Center once stood. My constant prayers are with all who have lost loved ones in this horrific tragedy, and with the courageous and enduring Americans that work daily in the ashes to level this mountain of sorrow, one shovel-full at a time.

YEARNING

45" x 36" Kanti Jocelyn Bisgaard
Zushi City, Kanagawa Prefecture Japan

This image came to me several days after the attack, while on a train travelling from Yokohama, to my home in a quiet Japanese seaside city. As suggested here, despite the explosion and the falling debris, people will always yearn for peace. The dove is incomplete, as is our peace.

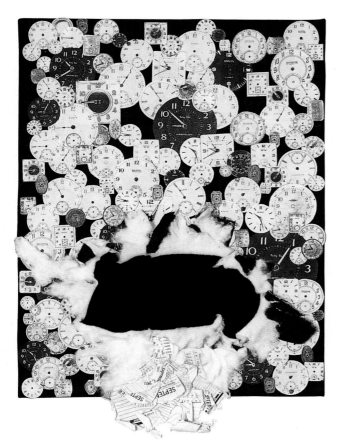

MARKING TIME

14" x 20" Robyn Daniel
Stow, MA USA

This piece was designed within 48-hours of the September 11th tragedy as a way for me to absorb the events and to begin to heal. It focuses on one moment that can change a way of life that can change a way of thinking that can make us look at our lives and our world. It is easy to believe we can envision the future, but something as big as an attack or as seemingly small as some other event can change our perception of our world. How do we see ourselves? How do we live in the same world when we've changed? What do we leave behind when we leave this world?

WHILE WE WERE ALL WATCHING

28" x 43½" Peggy Daley Spence
Tulsa, OK USA

On September 11, 2001, like many others I couldn't believe my eyes. The news got weirder—plane crash at the Pentagon, bombs at the White House. We were glued to the television until after midnight. This quilt is how I got through that awful day as the images were endlessly repeated on every channel. It happened right in front of us, while we watched.

The fabric with the watchful eyes has been in my stash for years— and it always made me feel uneasy. That day it called to me, as the news came over the airwaves and the rumors flew… I felt as though this image leapt into my hands—it nearly made itself. I wanted to record this feeling of being an immediate witness to such a horrible event.

What scares me most about the attacks is the egotism of the violence—"Believe the way we tell you to—or else!" That someone thinks they have the right to dictate my thoughts and actions, and is willing to kill themselves and anyone else in their way to make it so. That is truly evil. I do not condemn Muslims for these attacks. I blame the selfishness of fanatics, of every kind.

Terrorism Hits Home

14" x 17" Meena Schaldenbrand
Plymouth, MI USA

From the darkness of terror, patriotism reemerges as does unity, spirit of cooperation, determination to beat terrorism, strength, courage, kindness, faith and hope. So many ordinary people became extraordinary heroes and were truly inspiring. The Statue of Liberty reminds us of the wonderful freedoms we enjoy. The gun symbolizes violence and the devastating attack. The plane is a bomber instead of a 757 or 767. 911 is the date of the attack and also the phone number for help in an emergency...The zero of the 2001 has a TV antenna and the eyes of the world.

It has tears falling from them into the sea of grief and disbelief. The one has a cell phone for the revealing calls made. The 2001 is in a puzzle fabric. Why would anyone cause so much destruction on purpose? "No! No! No!" was our gut reaction as we felt shock, fear, anger, uncertainty, and grief.

No Terror, No Error

64" x 58" Ségolène Dianmant-Berger
Houston, TX USA

Deeply shocked by the September 11th tragedy, I wanted to express my support of the fight against terrorism, as well as my fear that an error could lead to an even bigger tragedy. I have surrounded the ruins of the World Trade Center in fabrics from five continents to illustrate the international aspect of this conflict.

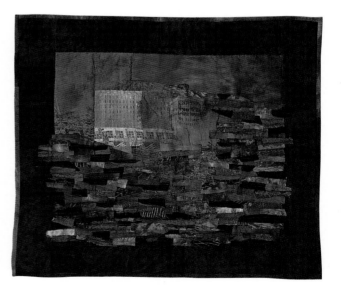

Ruins and Hope

30½" x 27" Navah Liberman
Ra'anana, Israel

Liberty will prevail!

For the spirit of man is stronger than terror, and the power of thought, creativity, and choice is stronger than any tyrant. Thus, fear no evil and pray for the best. And though the ruins are still burning, and the struggle may take time; tyrants will fall, justice will glow, and true peace will soon arrive.

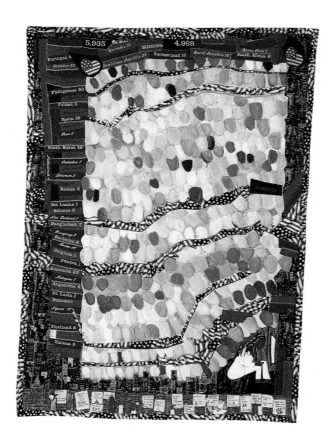

ALL THOSE PEOPLE

44" x 64½" Dindga McCannon
New York, NY USA

My daughter had a beautiful wedding on September 8th. Because I had cooked food for 100-plus people and the activities of the wedding, I was still too exhausted on September 11th to go down to my doctor's office (two blocks from the World Trade Center) that morning. As I walked the dog in Riverside Park suddenly I heard sirens... the sound wouldn't stop. They were racing downtown. When I came out of the park I noticed there were lots of cars exiting the highway. I asked a policeman what had happened and he said that a plane just flew into the World Trade Center. I started to pray. My quilt is a portrayal of me on that day watching the TV, too numbed and too nervous to move. The first thing I thought of was all those people who did go to the World Trade Center that day, those who will never come home…All I can do at this point is pray for all those affected and for world peace.

THE MEASURE OF STRENGTH IN ALL OF US

43" x 38" Laurie Sullivan
The Woodlands, TX USA

A giant tear is the backdrop of the torn buildings of people. My sadness for the victims, our country's loss of innocence and for the people who felt they had to resort to this level of violence. Hearts of love come up from the ruins. Love for the victims. Love for our fellow man. Hope flutters above. Ms. Liberty stands beside us as a reminder of our strength. United We Stand. Like a child's drawing, the Hands of brotherhood are colored the different colors of the human race, surrounded by a fragmented broken heart. The field of forget-me-not flowers are for the victims we shall never forget. Silver tears are scattered throughout the flowers as we will mourn our country's loss for a long time. The American flag waving around the quilt is stiff, representing the strength of our nation. It stands out to show our democracy and to show the world the measure of our strength.

WAVES

39" x 39" Beth Ann Carney
Yonkers, NY USA

I watched in horror as the world around me spiraled out of control. Explosions, dark, menacing clouds, gray sky, twisted metal and flames flickering. Wave after wave.

I watched the firemen and women, police, the paramedics, and volunteers arrive. I watched, I waited, I cried. Wave after wave.

I looked out my window and saw the candles flickering as flags waved in the wind. Our colors were standing strong and proud. Wave after wave.

Lower Manhattan was dark through the night. Lady Liberty was standing alone in the harbor. Her torch lit sending us a message of hope and strength. Wave after wave.

ONE NATION UNDER GOD

47½" x 47½" Marjorie A. Nelson
Frankfort, MI USA

When I think about all of the people that the events of September 11, 2001 have affected, these thoughts come to mind:

> *KEEP OUR FAITH*
>
> *STAND UNITED*
>
> *PRAY*

AMERICA'S HEART RAINS

33" x 48" Terry White
Rockport, IN USA

This is an image I couldn't get out of my head until I made it. I was profoundly shocked and experienced overwhelming sadness when I saw the events unfold on the television. I felt helpless except to pray and make this quilt and support my daughter, who is a brand new airman in the Air Force of the United States. This image represents America's sadness and love for the victims of the 911 attack. It also represents the prayers and necessary hope for recovery for us all.

EVIL LURKS IN THE SHADOWS

20½" x 27" Judy Kriehn
Garland, TX USA

Over the past few years, I've watched the news reports about "hate crimes"—skinheads defacing Jewish synagogues or burning the churches of African-American congregations, protestors firebombing medical clinics or assassinating doctors, and now Muslim extremists targeting Americans…

Oddly, despite the obvious dangers brought to light that fateful day, I have not felt any fear. Shock and disbelief, but not fear…

When I decided to make a 9/11/01 quilt, what you see here is the image that kept coming to mind–crimson reds, blacks, and shadowy sheers, with lots of jagged edges. The evening I sat down to make the top, I decided to approach it as a collage rather than a quilt. As I worked, and the visual images in the quilt began to appear, the more evident it became to me that this particular act of terrorism MADE ME MAD!!!…

THE AWAKENING

52" x 38" Arlene Blackburn
Millington, TN USA

As the bombing of Pearl Harbor and the assassination of JFK were to older generations of Americans, September 11, 2001 is a defining moment for a new generation of American youth. We were caught sleeping while wrapped in the comforts of the liberty and freedom that our country offers, only to be awakened by the horror and reality of terrorism.

The World in Flames

37½" x 53" Amira Wishinsky
Tel Aviv, Israel

As a citizen of a country suffering for many years from continuous terror, on September 11th I sat petrified in front of my TV set watching the second aircraft crash into the World Trade Center and both towers collapse. I felt as if the whole world was going down in flames. What will the future be like if they succeeded to hit so hard even the strong and peaceful United States? In the quilt I made, I tried to express my feelings while under the impression of the tragedy.

Response #1: Stunned

18" x 18" Caryl Bryer Fallert
Oswego, IL USA

Speechless. Can't believe my eyes. Shock.

After 28 years as a flight attendant, this is much too close.

Perspective and words of wisdom may come later.

I believe that beauty and love are the antidote to hate, so I will focus on beauty and love. I hope I'm right.

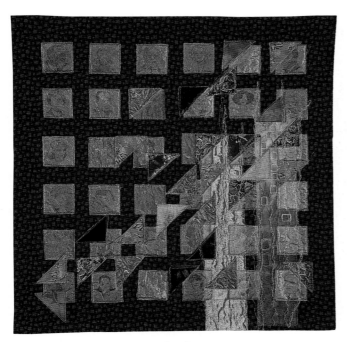

ASHES TO ASH: A 9/11/01 COMMEMORATION

30½" x 31" Christine Adams
Rockville, MD USA

My thoughts turn to the many families that have been directly affected by the events of 9/11. Tragedy is a great leveler; the famous and not so famous are treated the same. For weeks after the incidents in New York, Washington, D.C., and Pennsylvania, pictures of the missing were in newspapers, on makeshift bulletin boards, and in our hearts. It was important to me to capture both the fragility and beauty of life. Ashes to Ash is my way of commemorating those who died that day.

A TIME OF GIFTS

19" x 22" Ann McDermott
Oklahoma City, OK USA

This quilt was inspired by an article in the New York Times on September 26, 2001, written by Stephen Jay Gould, he states, "The tragedy of human history lies in the enormous potential for destruction in rare acts of evil, not in the high frequency of evil people. Complex systems can only be built step by step, whereas destruction requires but an instant. Thus, in what I like to call the Great Asymmetry, every spectacular incident of evil will be balanced by 10,000 acts of kindness, too often unnoted and invisible as the 'ordinary' efforts of a vast majority." In my quilt, the evil is represented by the large black square in the center and the multi-colored triangles represent the 10,000 acts of kindness.

TWO THOUSAND ONE, NINE ELEVEN

29¼" x 38¼" Sonja Tugend
Chagrin Falls, OH USA

As I neared completion of this quilt in early September, I struggled with its name. Usually by the time I'm halfway through a new piece, it tells me what its name is—for some reason it just wasn't happening this time.

I left early on the morning of September 11th to drive to Pittsburgh with two friends to attend the Fiberart International Exhibition…
As I returned home, the unnamed quilt on my design wall jolted me into reality. Staring me in the face were the images of flames and fractured windows that isn't what I saw when I finished working the night before! Unable to touch the quilt for days, I finally felt a ray of hope as I stitched the final few stitches onto my quilt: May the spark of hope stay alive in every heart.

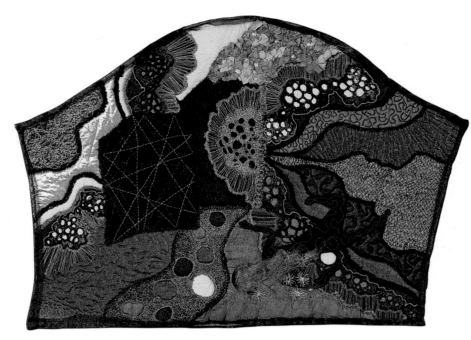

FROM EVIL COMES PROMISE FOR THE FUTURE

19" x 13" Linda Dawson
St. Petersburg, FL USA

As the towers burn, humanity lays prostrate. The rainbow of promise is in disarray, but a silver lining peeks through. Flowers from around the world say that humanity is not dead, she lives and, like the phoenix, will rise with promise for our future.

LIBERTY COMPROMISED

14" x 15" Frances Holliday Alford
Austin, TX USA

As chaos surrounds Manhattan, Lady Liberty stands eclipsed by smoke and shadows. Despite our despair, we stand united.

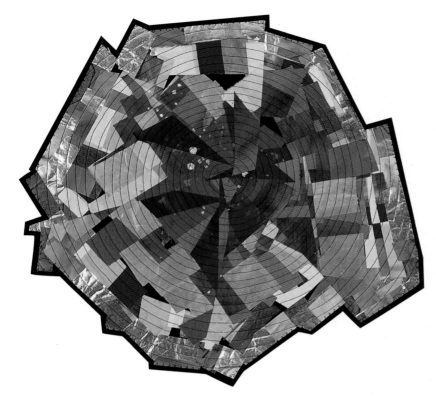

SHATTERED CHAKRAS

20" x 19" Emily Lewis
Cincinnati, OH USA

Before September 11, 2001, I had a quilt forming in my head that would illustrate the Chakras or energy centers in the body that connect with the physical, emotional and spiritual levels in the body represented by colors.

On September 13th, I went to the studio fully expecting to create the quilt the way I had been planning. I thought keeping myself busy would help me feel more normal. The first thing that changed was the shape. It decided to be circular. It also decided to be two quilts. Then the cuts began. Shattering the circle into smaller slices.Then it hit me. I was creating the Chakras of the explosion. The spiral seemed natural. This is one of two identical quilts, created at the same time. The image of the World Trade Center Towers collapsing will be etched on my mind for years to come...

BROKEN BUT UNBOWED

31" x 40" Heather Blair Pregger
The Woodlands, TX USA

Tuesday morning, early September. Finish breakfast. Stop at the market. Turn on the radio. Shock. Disbelief. In an instant the world has changed. Broken but Unbowed attempts to portray this shattering sense of change. A jarring, black over red fractured background represents the unimaginable physical and emotional devastation wrought by the attacks. Against the broken background, two black columns stand whole, symbolizing both the void left in the American fabric and the unbowed determination of the American spirit. From above, light begins to stream, penetrating and illuminating the darkness of ignorance and terror. Yet our perspective has been irrevocably altered; that we can no longer view life in a traditional fashion is reflected in the asymmetric border.

A World: Broken; A World : Healing

40" x 50" Dani McKenzie
Puyallup, WA USA

The images are intense. Palm Pilots and Analysis Reports that are mere flotsam and jetsam in the winds blowing through the corridors of Manhattan. Burning cairns of metal and concrete in NYC. Unstoppable tears from the eyes of a rescue worker upon finding a friend in the rubble. Torn earth and scattered plane fragments in Pennsylvania.

And yet, there are the stories. Images of soldiers draping a flag over the wound in the wall of the Pentagon. Spontaneous shrines…Heroic rescue efforts…volunteers from every religion guarding Mosques, immense outpouring of love and support from around the globe. And, maybe most importantly, we pulled together as a nation and began thinking of ourselves as Americans, regardless of our backgrounds. The world may have broken, but we were there to catch the pieces.

Day of Horror

47" x 52" Regina Seagrave
Bozeman, MT USA

I was attending a workshop by Joan Colvin the week of September 11, 2001. I love her beautiful, serene work representing nature, and I was eager to learn how to go about it. After the terrorist attack, after a long struggle to be calm, this explosion happened on the design wall. I see the fiery collapse of the Trade Center and the inferno with all the black smoke, ashes and dust and far-reaching consequences for our nation. This is my reaction to the day of horror. It was and still is a wrenching design to me. I hope the viewer understands that I didn't produce it lightheartedly.

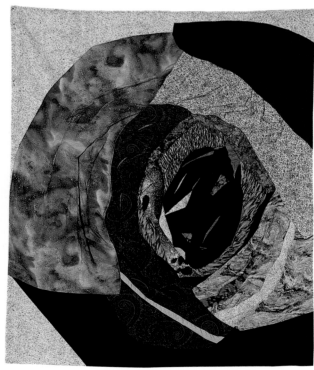

SHATTERED SYNAPSES

11½" x 9¼" Sandra Betts
Saint John, New Brunswick Canada

Shattered Synapses was created as a catharsis so I could clear my mind of all the numbing images of madness incarnate. How you perceive it will depend on whether you see it as falling into an abyss or rising above this awful madness.

The entire world as we have always known it has been shattered by the insanity of the events of 9/11—never again to be as we once knew. Can we rise above the shattering of our dreams of a life of contentment and freedom or will we fall deeper into the abyss of Shattered Synapses? This piece was done as a spontaneous cathartic reaction to the events of 9/11. My mind was reeling. I felt the depths of despair that humans visited these senseless actions upon fellow humans, innocent of any blame. GOD (by whatever name you are known) help us all.

LURKING: WE SHOULD HAVE KNOWN

53" x 59" Barbie Swanson
Pompano Beach, FL USA

I've always had a slightly uncomfortable feeling about today's communications since I spend much time on the internet. I began this quilt a couple years ago and put it away until sometime when I would feel more able to deal with these thoughts. The original title was to be simply: LURKING. It was meant to make people think about the dangers but not to specify an exact event. After the tragic events that began on September 11, 2001, I found that it was the time to bring this quilt back out and complete it. My constant thought was that we should have known that something was going on, that we had foregone some of the responsibility we have for each other, that we were so involved in our own environment that we forgot to look up and see that evil was lurking…I am still planning further work on this creation if history so dictates. Though I wish this were truly the end of the terrorism, I am not so confident that all their plans have been thwarted. My thoughts and sympathy go to all who have and will suffer from the tragedies of those unconscionable evil ones.

In Harm's Way

23" x 33" Rosemary Claus-Gray
Doniphan, MO USA

This quilt expresses my raw and tumultuous feelings after the terrorist attack on September 11, 2001, in America. I am outraged!...Innocent men, women, and children are in harm's way. The family in this quilt has drawn closer together due to danger surrounding them. They appear gray, as they are covered with the ashes of the fire. This family represents the vulnerable human-ness that is within all of us...Underneath our skin, we are all very much alike. Life may bring trial by fire to any of us at one time or another, sometimes in terrible ways, as in the horrifying terrorists attacks. Though in harm's way, some will survive. Courage, strength, faith, and our will to overcome will arise out of the ashes of this tragedy. Our unity has been tested, and has been found strong.

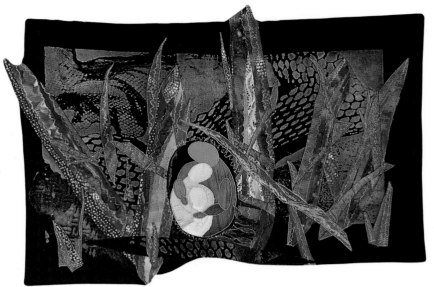

And the Trees cried, "Why can't we get along?"

27" x 41" Pamela R. Morris
Venice, FL USA

As I listened that horrible morning all I could think of was how we all share one world. Why does such hatred have to be present? I cannot understand how some people commit acts of violence towards one another in the name of God.

These hands on the quilt represent the three major religions, and how much I want them to reach towards each other for acceptance of differing viewpoints.

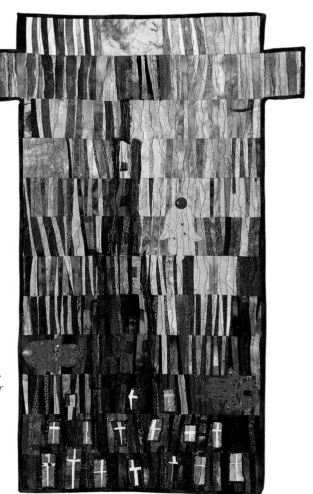

REQUIEM FOR LOST INNOCENCE

7½" x 10" Sandra Betts
Saint John, New Brunswick Canada

Requiem for Lost Innocence *is shaped like the human heart. It is broken, bleeding and on fire. Above the fires loom the images of World Trade Center. There are drops of blood and tears.*

I am Canadian. Few of us have no ties by blood or history to the USA. Today I am my American cousin. I mourn the loss of innocence, of naiveté that we could live a life of contentment and freedom in a world where we wished no harm to any other, to be able to render help where needed without the intention being misconstrued. I mourn the loss of the idea that we live in a safe sane world of tolerance and freedom, isolated from the madness infecting so many other places in the world. I weep for the innocents lost on this terrible day, September 11, 2001.

GRIEF

24" x 36" Julie Brook Alexander
Houston, TX USA

On the morning of September 11th, two stacks left from delightful projects sat on my sewing table…Transfixed by the terrorist attacks, I combined these two reminders of happier times into a project expressing my sense of loss. This quilt reflects the stages of my grief. Bright, varied scraps bound by wide, jagged stitches convey the sense of shock at the events. Anger reveals itself as razor slashes made into the surface. Stitching the bright pieces onto and through the quilt conveys the feeling of a world out of balance. Lastly, grief appears as a veil of black dye. Grief transforms the blue sky and the colorful patches into a subdued, somber scene.

When I made this quilt, I made it without knowledge of this exhibit. I simply responded to the September tragedy. I hope that you notice something I observed when readying it for exhibition. Small bits of pure color shine through the black dye—in spite of a deep sense of communal loss, I reserved a place for hope.

MOON IN MY WINDOW

24" x 18" Mona Tolin
Tustin, CA USA

Moon in My Window—*the terrorists cannot take it away from my soul. I dreamed I stood in my window and saw the devastation in New York. The world cried for those who were lost and the moon shed my tears. Like the moon, America stands solid and determined to be strong … The three tiny birds in the sky represent to me the holy trinity—Father, Son and Holy Ghost—who are lifting the souls of those who died and the spirits of those who lived. My heart cried out "Why? Dear God, why?" My soul cries every night.*

BUT THE DOOR NEVER OPENED...

11½" x 17" Amy Koester
Palm Coast, FL USA

Watching the events of September 11, 2001 unfold I saw many vivid images that will be forever in my memory. Images of smoke, flames, rubble, people covered with dust, the skeleton of the towers after they fell—all influenced this work.

I'm a mother and my heart broke when I heard stories of children in day care centers whose mommies didn't come to pick them up at the end of the day. More than any other image, written on my heart is the one I only imagine: a child waiting at a door that doesn't open, for a mom or dad that will never return.

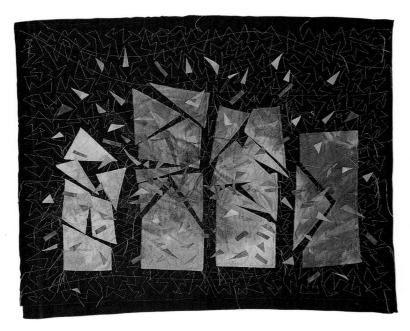

9-11: SHATTERED

42" x 33½" Sherrie Spangler
Rockford, IL USA

I painted the fabric for Shattered the night before the September 11, 2001 terrorist attacks. I had intended to have the fabric represent clouds and leaves and was going to call the piece Blown Away. After watching in horror as coverage of the attacks unfolded on television Tuesday morning, my gut reaction was to slash the fabric, quickly arrange it on a field of black and fracture the piece with jagged quilting lines. The four columns represent the shattered buildings and bodies in the World Trade Center towers, the Pentagon and the Pennsylvania field. The quilting lines speak of our country's overall sense of security being shattered.

GOD BLESS THE WORLD

36" x 36" Stephanye Schuyler
Eliot, ME USA

First you cry.

Then you give money.

Then you quilt.

I had to do something, and quilting was my outlet. The fire block poured out, and I completed it in the weekend. But the quilt felt dark and incomplete. The second block, muted and mournful, is also hopeful, as it expresses my prayer of peace for the world.

WISH YOU WERE HERE

40" x 32" Lauren McCarthy Works
Ann Arbor, MI USA

On September 11th, an entire zip code ceased to exist. In the New York Times, regular advertisements were pulled for a time; while individuals, companies, organizations and countries paid homage to the heroes and the lost. The outpouring of solidarity and sympathy was both heartening and heart-wrenching. I tore out many of these pieces and hung them on the refrigerator. The words helped some-what. More time is needed to heal. My hope for the future is in the lower left corner: shalom (Hebrew for peace).

Acknowledgments: the Ghandi quote is from a piece placed in the Times by Iris Cantor the column on the quilt back is by Leonard Pitts of the Miami Herald. Thanks to the Ann Arbor Stadium Post Office employees for help with the postcard. And to Larry for a shoulder to cry on.

THE TREE OF LIFE

18" x 30" Bret Adams
Fischer, TX USA

I am sure my response to the events of September 11th was very similar to that of most Americans. I felt insecure in a way I had never felt before and the more I heard on the newscasts those first few hours, the more I reacted with concern, fear, and outrage...I decided that I wanted my quilt to reflect my hope that we would continue to move forward seeing the best possible outcomes for our nation and the world. I chose to use words and an image that had particular impact from those newscasts to convey my feelings as we moved up from initial reactions to the tributes to the heroes...As individuals our greatest personal achievements are usually prompted by enormous challenges that certainly do not appear as gifts when we are confronted by them. I believe that the human race is being offered the same opportunity for growth and it is up to all of us to continue moving toward peace and equity on a worldwide level for us to truly take from this tragedy what is possible, and necessary. I hope my quilt will remind us of our potential and how powerful we, as a people, are when we determine the direction we chose to go.

SUNBONNET SUE IN NEW YORK, SEPTEMBER 2001

16" x 34" Kim Bunchuck
Greenport, NY USA

The top block of this quilt was finished in August. It was made for an Internet block swap in which Sunbonnet Sue was to be represented in each of the fifty states. For the New York block, I chose to show Sunbonnet Sue embarking on an adventure to New York City, using the lower Manhattan skyline, featuring, the World Trade Center, for the background.

After the attack, I posted the block on sunbonnetsue.com my website and asked the other contributors their opinion on whether or not to change the image. Without exception, everyone wanted to keep the Twin Towers in the block.

This small remembrance quilt of September 2001 depicts the way New York was at the beginning of September (top block), September 11th (middle block), and the days following when New Yorkers gathered around the "wall of prayers" (bottom).

We will never forget.

GIULIANI: THE KING OF HEARTS FOR NEW YORK CITY SEPTEMBER 11, 2001

21" x 15" Susanne Hinzman
Bethesda, MD USA

During this unbelievable trauma, Mayor Giuliani has shown total class and seemingly unending energy. His entire focus has been New York City—its people, its firefighters, its rescue workers and their dogs, its police force —in its recovery. His calm and thoughtful manner has helped all those affected...This quilt is dedicated to Mayor Giuliani and all of the firefighters, police, and rescue workers and their dogs. In this quilt, I hope that you see the three aspects shown: the tall towers, Giuliani's name, and the flag. I hope that you sense the emotional trauma and the blood, sweat, and tears that I felt in making this, one of many social commentary quilts I have done. God Bless America!

The Monster of 9-11

52" x 39" Carla Gulati
Nicasio, CA USA

I am astonished that one mean and cruel individual, who supposedly lives his life in caves, could conceive of this horrific plan to bring death and suffering to so many Americans. What a coward to spend his life in hiding and convince weak, spineless, and hopeless people to do his bidding. My quilt is a composite of The Monster conceiving of the idea to blow up the Twin Towers and the Pentagon. There is fire everywhere. Fear of anthrax is growing. We are at war in Afghanistan, hunting down a coward.

The hatred is to be buried, and forgiveness and love must be nurtured in all of us that remain.

The Day that Time Stood Still

37" x 23½" Mary Ellen Landry
Houma, LA USA

The dark figure represents all the victims of 9/11. It is seen against white depicting the afterlife. The silver grid stands for the Twin Towers. Red symbolizes fire and explosions. The beading represents rocks and debris falling everywhere. The red borders (clocks with wings) say time stood still.

Message on quilt: Tho I am gone from this earth I live in peace with the Light.

Because of so much destruction I had to fracture my quilt top to feel better. I did.

Note: Even the birds on the farm didn't fly or sing that day.

ELEGY: BIG AND SMALL

15" x 15" Virginia A. Spiegel
Nebraska City, NE USA

Elegy: Big and Small *was made in one day as an elegy not only for the fabric of our society now—unalterably rent by the events of September 11, 2001—but—also for the great loss to us all of individuals who were mothers, fathers, daughters, sons, wives, husbands, lovers, and friends.*

WHAT COLOR IS THE SOUL?

45" x 40" Norma DeHaven
Fitchburg, WI USA

This piece began as a color study—trying to develop an overlay of the primary and secondary colors based on a basic block design. It grew into something much more symbolic and healing—the colors of the work represent all the people of the world, mingled and overlapping. The black-and-white diagonal inner border slices into the work representing the realities of living in today's difficult times. The symbolism of the white background is somewhat self-explanatory. I found comfort in these sayings and wanted to highlight them—but I also wanted to indicate that we do have a buffer between the cold hard realities of the world and the intricacies of our souls—our faith, our family, and our friends.

Transformation Scene

12" x 18" Rosemary Eichorn
Soquel, CA USA

In the aftermath of the terrorist attacks on NYC and the Pentagon, my first thoughts were that I could only deal with the events if I worked out my feelings through my art. As I considered what I might do, my energy waned and any ideas I had only seemed to trivialize the tragedy, so I shelved the project. Weeks later, while attempting to bring order to my studio, I procrastinated, deciding instead to see what would happen if I transferred images to sheer silk. Looking closely at the horrific specter of the WTC, I saw an angel's image in the billows of smoke! In my heart, I felt this image transforming the energy of the event…I only needed to show up for the artwork to reveal itself. Even in quickly finishing the piece as time was running out, I decided to paint into the border to see what might happen. The paint spread into the artwork with a mind of its own, creating the illusion of a shaft of light focused on the angel. When I looked up the meaning of the word transformation*, I found a reference to the transformation scene. The transformation scene is when a curtain is dropped in theatrical performances, changing the circumstances of the drama. The art and its name were gifted through me. The transformation will continue to reveal its expression in all of our lives with the passage of time.*

OUR HUMANITY MUST TRIUMPH IN SPITE OF INHUMANITY

22¼" x 31" Nancy Schlegel
Castleton, NY USA

The title of this quilt came from a fellow quilter, Kanti Jocelyn, and gave me a way of coping with this tragedy. It allowed me to focus on all the people in New York City, around the country and even around the world who gave their time, their money, their blood and even their lives in helping their fellow men instead of destroying them. The image of the skeleton of the towers is a memorial to all who lost their lives there. The silhouettes of the firefighters of New York City, the man extending a glass of water to all those who had to walk miles from the destruction and the man giving blood are representative of these many caring people. The eagle flying overhead is crying in despair but is still strong and proud.

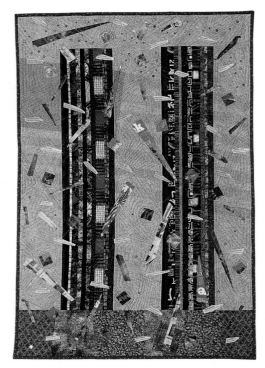

TRIBUTE: TWO

28" x 40" Cathy Neri
Shenorock, NY USA

In my twenty-five years as a quilter, I have always found myself drawn to abstract shapes and vibrant hues and colors. So much of our world changed on September 11th. When I was finally able to return to my studio and work again with fabric, this quilt was my reaction to those changes in our world.

I've been collecting fabric in blacks, grays, and somber colors for years without knowing what I would do with them. Color aside, there is a lot of symbolism in this quilt, not the least of which is represented by the shards of treated and stitched paper and newsprint including items from the New York Times' Portraits of Grief pages …As quilters, we have the power to help mend the world, one stitch at a time.

LINGERING IMAGES

40" x 30" D.L. Folz
Hudson, WI USA

On the morning of September 11th, I watched all the horrors unfold on TV. For three days I watched everything. Then, for my own sanity I couldn't watch any longer. I wanted to forget, only I couldn't. Images of what I saw haunted me.

I couldn't not make this quilt.

FROM THE RUBBLE...

18½" x 18½" Katherine Stubbs Ward
Riviera Beach, FL USA

As I watched events unfold from the horror of September 11th, I was struck by the coming together of this nation. We have so many differences—ethnic, religious, lifestyle, standards of living—that the sense of community has been lost. As people reacted to the events of that day, it became evident that underneath all our differences we are still a nation that can come together in times of trouble and help each other, that sense of community is still there, sometimes well hidden, but ready to grow when needed!

*I wish for a world where
hate is taught no longer.*

TOGETHER WE STAND

35" x 31" Elaine Martin
North Platte, NE USA

There are many ways that we, as American people, have weathered the shock, the grief, the terrible losses, and the massive invasion of our lives caused by the September 11, 2001, terrorist airplane bombings in New York, Washington, D.C., and Pennsylvania.

I made a quilt. It has been very difficult to erase the repeated televised events from my mind. As an artist might reach for paint and brush, a quilt artist reaches for fabric and thread. I chose colors and fabric motifs to mirror my feelings, used harsh design lines, and stitched radical quilting to express my fears and hopes. As a nation, we have been changed forever, but together we will stand, the United States of America, and the individuals that are her people.

GROUND ZERO

52" x 38" Marion Mackey
West Chester, PA USA

On September 11, 2001, we watched the television, unable to turn away, transfixed by the image playing over and over before our eyes. This horrific viewing of burning buildings, fluttering papers, and brilliant sky had burned itself into my mind. Within a day or two, the image began to emerge in fabric as skyscrapers appeared, then, clear blue sky and terrible burning buildings complete with flames. Below the World Trade Center the bright yellow clothing of the rescue workers brought control to the chaotic scene. Yet, our spirit is undaunted, our patriotism is solid and the flag still flies over all. This quilt is dedicated to the victims and the rescue workers.

RISING FROM THE RUBBLE

65" x 43" Joan McGinnis
Powell, TN USA

Across the face of this quilt, lie the ruins of the field in Pennsylvania, the scarred and broken Pentagon in Washington, D.C. and the crumbled remains of the World Trade Center in New York City. The scenes blend into each other, as the horror reached across the whole of humanity that terrible day. Lying in the ashes and rubble, the four dark, burnt butterflies represent the four aircraft that went down during the attacks…The quilting in the border is jagged and uneven, representing the shock and anger we have all felt. In the clear blue sky, the beading represents the souls of those who perished during this horrendous attack rising towards heaven…Begun just four days after the attack, this quilt was made because it had to be made, not simply for inclusion in a show…May God bless us in these dark days of national grief and may we be touched by His healing love in the days of turmoil ahead.

IN THE DARKNESS

28" x 34" Karen Cote
Pittsford, NY USA

On September 11th, pacing, I was suddenly overcome with the need to do something…So I started—first, the towers themselves, cloaked in smoke then bursting into flame. Then the people who watched from the streets in disbelief, then horror, throwing up their hands and trying in vain to hold up the buildings collapsing before their eyes. Those memorable hands can be seen in the border—first reaching upward, then clenched into angry fists. Open and raised in despair, and then, at the very top reaching gently to touch and guide the released souls of the victims, represented by iridescent butterflies. A quote from my favorite book, A Wrinkle in Time *by Madeline L'Engle, stuck in my head and gave me hope: "And the light shineth in the darkness, and the darkness comprehendeth it not." …*

ASHES TO ASHES DUST TO DUST

32" x 41" Claire Fenton
Houma, LA USA

I started this quilt a few days after 9/11. I could not sit and watch TV without doing something. It reflects the emotions I felt as I watched buildings, lives, and our sense of safety crumble before my eyes. Each embroidered cross represents lives lost…lives shattered. The magnitude of that day is still incomprehensible to me. This is my memorial to those innocent victims—unknowing heroes to us all.

NEW YORK: DAY 3

24½" x 43½" Kim Jalette
Laytonsville, MD USA

Like millions of Americans, I was riveted to the pictures on TV after the horrific terrorist acts. By the third day, the overriding images from New York were; ash, grayness, ghostly broken buildings with black holes where the window glass was once. This is what stayed with me…Not directly shown on TV, but only left to us to imagine there had been a person, an individual, a human being, behind each of those windows on the morning of September 11, 2001.

LOVE LIFTS US UP WHERE WE BELONG

54" x 35" Sharon Torregrosa
Trenton, MI USA

The events of September 11th moved me to create something tangible that would comfort me, and perhaps provide comfort to others. I have always been moved by the works of political cartoonists, when I found an image created by Mr. Bill Day, I knew that I had found my inspiration. When giving his permission for me to use his work, Mr. Day said that he was "honored..." but the honor is mine. My quilt is dedicated to the everyday heroes of September 11, 2001.

FLIGHTS OF ANGELS GUIDE THEE TO THY REST

25" x 14" Susan Brewer
Gaithersburg, MD USA

Like so many others, I sat transfixed with horror as the replay of the planes crashing into the towers filled my television screen. Then our local news station broke in to report that a third plane had crashed into the Pentagon, less than 20 miles away. I watched both towers crumble. My heart went numb. The tears flooding my face could not begin to reflect the awful silence echoing in my soul... That night, when I was finally able to drag myself away from the news, as I tried again to pray, I heard a voice calling me to join it. I passed into a trance. Suddenly my soul was dancing in a slow, steady circle around the remains of the World Trade Center along with hundreds, maybe even thousands, of other souls and angels. We were there to aid with the transition of the souls who had died, to provide comfort for those few who still lived, and protect the men and women working so diligently to rescue surviving victims. Two other times in the following week I was called to dance in that circle of love. I have no words to describe the experience, the knowing that we are so deeply loved, that no one dies alone, that God, Love-Manifest, cherishes each one of us. And so I quilted the angels, diving into the fires, protecting other buildings, guiding souls to heaven, shouting love into the heart of madness...They are with us always. Dedicated in love to those who lost their lives and to those who grieve the loss, and in a special way to those whose last moments were spent offering aid and comfort to those around them.

INNOCENCE LOST, UNITY FOUND

22" x 36" Phyllis Lee Nelms
McAlester, OK USA

While thinking about this quilt, the two images that haunted me were the Statue of Liberty, looking over the tragedy, and the unbelievably stark sadness of the skeletal remains of the World Trade Center.

On September 11, we lost not only some wonderful people and two majestic buildings, we lost our innocence; But we gained the unity of our Country again.

Sue carries Liberty's torch, remembering those she loves, and vows to be brave and stalwart, honoring those who died. Out of sadness and grief, we can find ways of never forgetting—and ways of bonding together under Lady Liberty's still-glowing torch.

WHERE'S MY MOMMY?

36" x 48" Liz Copeland
Bellevue, WA USA

The terrorist attacks on September 11th were overwhelming; too much to comprehend at one time. I found myself focusing on details as they were reported in the news. But by the end of the day, what I was focusing on was the lack of information about the children of the people who died in the attack. Who was picking them up from school? How many of them lost a parent that day? I found this remained the part that I could not let go of, so when this opportunity to make a quilt in reaction to this awful event arose, I had to deal with the image of loss that would not leave me. By making this quilt and another one to go to the Linus Project, I have started to move on. But I know that we, as a community, will be called on to help these children for years to come.

JUSTICE

36" x 36" Debi Harney
Puyallup, WA USA

On September 11th all of our lives changed dramatically. We will all remember where we were and what we were doing; but will we remember the emotions we experienced as we sat glued to our televisions? Will we remember the disbelief, the despair, the horror, and the hope?

Websters' says that justice, "is the principle or ideal of just dealing or right action." As I stitched on this quilt I was trying to heal my heart. I was stitching up the shattered belief I had of my safe and just place in the world.

With each stitch I became more and more convinced that justice will prevail and that the right action will be done. We, as a nation, will come together and defeat the hatred. I believe this to be a right action, a justice.

EIGHT OF HEARTS

15" x 21" Sheila Berman
Bethesda, MD USA

My local quilt group, Nimble Fingers, was doing a playing card challenge like the "Playing with a Full Deck Exhibit" which has been touring the country. Cards were dealt out last spring so each member could interpret her card in fabric. I spent the summer waiting to be inspired about my card, the eight of hearts. I finally got started in September and was working on it September 11, when my husband called to tell me turn on the television, something terrible was happening. I no longer felt like working on the clever design I had planned, so I cut into all the hearts I had prepared. Over the next few days, as I watched as much television coverage as I could stand, I made a new background for them. Although I had lived in New York, I was lucky not to have lost any friends or family—but it seems that none of us could really remain untouched by the tragedy or its aftermath.

LOYALTY

22" x 18" Marla Wyant
Arlington, TX USA

Is this doggie preparing for the grueling task of a rescue worker?

Is this doggie waiting for his beloved companion?

Is this doggie suddenly homeless?

Remember all of our loved ones. 9/11/2001

HEROES

56" x 24" Brooke Flynn
Billings, MT USA

One of the good things to come out of the horror of September 11, 2001 is an affirmation that ordinary Americans are capable of both great compassion and incredible courage. The passengers on United Flight 93 were just ordinary business people and vacationers. Realizing what the hijackers had planned, they acted to save those on the ground. They were successful in saving their country additional grief and loss. How we wish they had been successful in saving themselves. I first pictured this quilt in blacks and reds; symbolizing anger, fear and pain. As I worked, I realized I really wanted to use "patriotic" colors. The quilting pattern symbolizes laurel leaves, which the ancient Greeks used to honor their heroes. God Bless the heroes of Flight 93—God Bless America!

A Passing Shadow

48" x 55" Diane Herbort
Arlington, VA USA

My home is just up the road from the Pentagon. I felt compelled to record the events of September 11, hoping, in part, to make some sense from seemingly senseless acts, and also, to exorcise the demons that have haunted me since that day. Working on this quilt reminded me that solace can be found in creativity... Mostly, I am haunted by the specter of that airplane, and an awareness of the passengers in the last terrifying moments of their lives. In my nightmares, the airliner has become the Angel of Death. I pray for the souls of everyone.

Stolen Lives

18" x 28" Maria Elkins
Dayton, OH USA

I watched in horror, over and over again throughout the day, as the two airplanes crashed into the World Trade Center on September 11, 2001. I was heartsick. Awful feelings swept over me: Dismay, disbelief, revulsion, shock, grief. I kept thinking about all the people in those buildings and on those airplanes. How could anyone do that to another human being? The image of the towers as two people filled my mind and wouldn't leave; symbols of the lives that were callously snatched away, leaving behind families with gaping holes.

What Happened?

25" x 17" Chris Wyant (Age 11)
Arlington, TX USA

I was inside the classroom when a teacher walked in. Then we all went to another teacher's room and saw the second plane crashing through the World Trade Center on television. I thought, "What's going on?" I had to watch the news to find out. They showed replays of it happening over and over and over. I wanted it all to stop.

Rise and Shine

36" x 31" Sandy Keating
Portland, OR USA

My heart has broken for the losses we have all had to face since September 11th. By writing my feelings directly onto the silk flag fabric, I was attempting to express the personal ownership I now feel toward the flag and all it represents. The stitching of the Statue of Liberty portrays the ideals of freedom and liberty. She stands in the harbor, reminding us of the hope and promise of our American dreams. The process of creating this quilt has helped me begin to heal. May you find some healing in viewing it.

BLOOD, SWEAT, AND TEARS— A TRIBUTE

40" x 30" Judith Matthews
Clovis, NM USA

The quilt was conceived in pain, born of love and grew from my heart. The red symbolizes courage; the blue, justice; and the white, purity. The torn edges of the white stripes represent the bandages that have helped the injured, and that will help bind our country together. The drops are for our tears and the blood, which has been splashed across our flag. The black binding, though a little frayed, is to show our grief, but also to show the strength that will surround and bind us as a nation in the days and years to come. The single star is for the United States of America, a shining star, surrounded by the fifty stars representing each state, coming together as one, in unity and love. The poppies are for remembrance for those who died, for those injured, and for the many who with their blood, sweat, and tears, have given so much of themselves. In God We Can Only Trust.

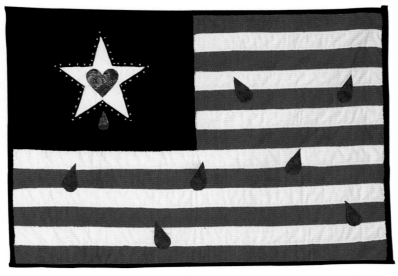

THE FLAME OF HOPE

19" x 13½" Amy Stewart Winsor
Cary, NC USA

In the aftermath of September 11th, I was haunted by the faces of the victims' spouses which I saw on TV. Each was frantically clinging to hope, hour after hour, day after day, waiting for news that her husband was still alive. At first their hope was strong, but gradually they had to face the realization that their loved ones were among the dead. At that moment, dreams of the future went up in smoke. The foundations of their lives fell away. The flame of hope went out.

AMERICA, 9-11-01, A NEW DAY OF INFAMY

33¼" x 33¼" Ann Kreutz
Aurelia, IA USA

...When designing my quilt for this exhibit, I decided to use some of the fabrics that I purchased on a shop hop. Ten of the fabrics in this quilt are from that trip.

I wanted to catalog the events of that day, as well as commemorate some of the people and slogans that have become well known since September 11. The cross is the primary means of comfort, for not only me, but for many of the accounts of the families I have read about. Our faith in Christ sustains and saves us. Our leaders have taken a tragic situation and shown their true leadership capabilities. We should all be proud of them. Let us all pray: God Bless America!

NEVER FORGET

36" x 41" Andrea Stern
Chauncey, OH USA

I have been in a state of numbness since the events of September 11th. The grid of the fallen towers and the blossoming of our flag across the local landscape have been the two images, which have burned themselves into my memory during the past month…This piece brings together the image of the building along with our flag and my memories of that morning. The red bars with the story in the background represent the joy of the morning; the blue grid, the terror of the events. The white stars represent our fellow Americans who died that day—as well as my hope for a better tomorrow for those left behind, and our world as a whole. The quilt is not heavily embellished, and its stark, graphic qualities represent the numbness and shock I felt that day, and am still feeling.

AMERICA IN MOURNING

10½" x 17¾" Rosemary Claus-Gray
Doniphan, MO USA

September 11, 2001

FRAGMENTED FLAG

**42" x 72" Kaffe Fassett, Liza Prior Lucy,
Bobbi Penniman**
New Hope, PA USA

Mosaic piecing expresses my feeling of fragility and vulnerability of this country after appearing so invincible. Arriving from England after the disaster, I was struck by the blossoming of Old Glories on every building and many cars. The shattered lives and windows resulting from the Towers are echoed in the fractured mosaic shards.—Kaffe Fassett

FREEDOM DID NOT DIE

36" x 30" Joanne M. Raab
Clarkson Valley, MO USA

September 11, 2001 was the first anniversary of my father's death. A very sad day for me, but my pain would be turned into a tiny speck in an ocean of grief as the day unfolded. Too horrible to imagine...now many would feel the same way I do about that day in September. Both 9/11/2000 and 2001 are forever joined together for me. The flames and chaos are slowly transformed into calm and understanding. This small poem has helped me work through both events by painting and sewing what I feel it gives me comfort, peace and hope.

911 AMERICA

11¾" " x 18" Marilyn Eimon
N. Easton, MA USA

Troubled by the September 11th disasters at the World Trade Center in NYC, the Pentagon in Washington D.C. and the downed plane in Pennsylvania, I needed to express my sadness and grief through my quilting. I tracked down the red and white striped fabric, bought so many years ago and stashed somewhere. With its uneven wavy stripes which seemed appropriate for a shaken nation...I planned to make fifty tears, one for each state. In the end I decided on only four tears to represent the devastation and sorrow resulting from the four crashed hijacked planes.

WITHOUT MALICE

24" x 36" Margaret Hunt
Clarks Hill, SC USA

Starting with the draping of the Pentagon with an enormous American flag, I have been repeatedly struck by the great beauty of all the American flags displayed in every conceivable place and manner. From the jaunty flags in the hard hats of the World Trade Center construction workers, to the majesty of the enormous flags floating in the breeze, I have tried to capture the feeling that these flags have evoked in me—both the patriotism and the courage of the American people. I also chose the flag as a symbol for the compassion and caring shown for the victims and their families since the September 11th tragedy—and for the courage and unity of the American people to do whatever must be done so that a September 11th will never happen again.

A Sorrow Shared...

16½" x 16½" Pamela Davis
Grand Forks, ND USA

Quilting is healing to the soul, as I and many other members of our North Star Quilters Guild discovered after our homes, our businesses, and our lives were swallowed by the icy waters of the Red River in 1997. As the waters receded and we returned to our homes, lives changed forever, we were challenged by our guild to tell the saga of our adventures through the medium of quilting…Now as I watch those affected by the bombings trying to piece back together their fractured lives, I cry a little, then pick up my palette, in this case a stash of fabric, and begin the process all over again. Piece by piece, I recreate something I have never seen, yet am touched by nonetheless. The healing begins. May this quilt touch your heart and bind you to those who have suffered. A sorrow shared is a burden lightened.

A Sad Day: 09/11/01

28" x 18" Helia Rendon
Sunrise, FL USA

I was at work when I heard the news…I could not believe one of the tallest buildings I remember so well from my visit to New York, now had a gaping hole in it. All I could see was black smoke pouring out. It just couldn't be true. Then the second tower was hit. The reality of it being a terrorist attack struck me like a bolt of lightning. To make matters worse, the towers collapsed. I was sad, confused, scared, and very angry.

Quilt work is how I express and share my feelings with others. The heart stands for those we lost in the attack that day. The flag symbolizes everyone in this beautiful country who, in one way or another, has been affected by this tragedy. I am still very sad, confused, scared, and angry, but this is America and we will survive.

God Bless America.

FREEDOM OF THE SKIES

22¼" x 18½" Beej Neal
Coshocton, OH USA

Freedom of the Skies *was created in remembrance of the passengers and crew of the four planes that crashed on September 11, 2001; Flight 11, Flight 175, Flight 77, and Flight 93.*

It is also in remembrance of the many others who died as a result of the orchestrated collisions at the Twin Towers, the Pentagon, and in rural Pennsylvania.

Hand sewing this quilt provided an outlet to ponder and grieve the inestimable losses of September 11, 2001. May America once again have freedom of the skies.

Your creativity mirrors the spirit of America—thank you!

NEW TEARS

24" x 30" Kim Ritter
Houston, TX USA

Tears that burst from my eyes were unlike any I had ever shed before— sad, angry, jagged, unbelieving.

REMEMBER

31" x 35½" Susan Victoria
Ashway, RI USA

In memory of all the people whose lives have been devastated or destroyed as a result of the terrorist activity on 9/11/2001. May God bless all of you! In place of the blue field with white stars, I used fabric that depicts New York City and the World Trade Center twin towers. I placed eleven flags in that field; nine of the flags are in the form of stars (9/11). Out of the flames (quilted) is born the American bald eagle, as a symbol of our fierce patriotism. He cries a tear of blood. The quilt is bordered in black to symbolize our grief. Completed in 1½ days.

TERROR

44" x 27½" Andi Perejda
Arroyo Grande, CA USA

The tension and anxiety felt by our nation on September 11, 2001 is depicted on the face of Old Glory. The stripes form knots which can be interpreted by each in his own way. Knots may depict fear, bandages, unity of purpose, or cohesiveness. Birds replace stars in the field of blue…Words from the Pledge of Allegiance are quilted into the background, reminding us that, we are a diverse, pluralistic populace that comprises one nation. We must protect our unique freedoms. The skyline of New York City is missing its twin towers in the lower right corner and the perfect binding usually found here is shattered. We are exposed. What is the fabric of our nation?

OUT OF THE DEPTHS OF MY SOUL I CRIED

47" x 32" Karen Boutte
Benicia, CA USA

On 9/11, I was awakened by a phone call from my husband, "Honey, turn on the TV and call me back." That was the beginning of the nightmare that still keeps playing in my head. I watched the news in horror as the World Trade Center crumbled. People running for their lives down streets no longer familiar. I watched, I cried, and I screamed as the smoke and flames from New York, The Pentagon, and a field in Pennsylvania lay in rubble. I sewed and cried and continued to put fabric on my design wall as this quilt made itself. I was just the messenger.

My tears are for the tremendous loss of life and innocence. The souls of those gone too soon amid the smoke and rubble will remain in my memory forever. Lest We Forget, not likely.

SORROW WALKS

11" x 12" Maxine Farkas
Lowell, MA USA

Sorrow walks with broken wings through silent canyons of dust torn dreams

QUILT OF COMPASSION

104" x 84" Laura Fogg and Betty Lacy
Ukiah, CA USA

Thank you to the Members of the Mendocino Quilt Artists Group: Ann Horton, Joyce Paterson, Marilyn Simpson, Leila Kazimi, Dede Ledford, Carla DeCrona, Susan Blue, MaryAnn Michelsen, Lynn Harris, and Vicky Groom. Ukiah friends and neighbors Ukiah, CA.

Nine days after the tragedy on September 11th, Betty called Laura to say, "I want to make a quilt." Laura's response was, "Me too, but I've been utterly paralyzed." With the idea on the table and our emotions unleashed, images of the horror, chaos and devastation came pouring out of our souls. We worked almost wordlessly, crying and ripping fabric as we began to express what we felt.

As we worked through the unmentionable pain, we began to talk of compassion and hope and spirituality. Members of our quilt group started coming by with ideas and offerings. Pieced crosses, handmade flowers, candles, flags, and images of deities and spiritual leaders from around the world were added to the border. Friends and neighbors dropped in as the word about our quilt spread, and the border grew yet again.

People who did not have things to give found other ways to contribute—they brought food, ran errands, and even showed up at midnight to give the tired quilters shoulder and neck massages. They cheered us on and gave us hugs. We ultimately realized that the subject of our quilt was no longer the central scene of horror, but the surrounding universal prayer for compassion. It is a work of love. After nine unbelievably intense days from start to finish, our quilt was ready to be shown to the world. We hope its message will be seen and understood by many.

FRACTURED SKY/HALLOWED GROUND

22½" x 34½" Dana Lacy Chapman
Plano, TX USA

On September 11, 2001, at home, alone, I turned on the radio. The unspeakable horror that met my ears! I kept waiting for an Orwellian "just a story" disclaimer, as when the Martian invasion was reported over the radio at Halloween so many years ago. I turned on the television, and, juxtaposed with a perfect autumn day, this image fractured the sky, and burned my soul…When the towers came down, and all those sparks of humanity, bravery, courage were snuffed out; when the smoke and dust finally cleared enough a second image emerged. The rust colored steel skeleton stood in homage, cathedral like in appearance, marking this sight as hallowed…

WEEP FOR THE WORLD

24" x 19" Marilyn Studholme
East Lothian, Scotland, UK

In a few shocking moments the world suddenly became a grayer place. My first thoughts, watching the same images repeated over and over again, was just how much these tragic deaths would affect not only the American nation, but the rest of the world too.

Mourn for the dead. Cry for a nation.

Weep for the world. There must be hope. There must.

STICKS AND STONES

12" x 14" Mary Jo Bowers
Chicago, IL USA

The daily images of the destruction by the terrorists compelled me to do my own image of what happened on 9/11/01. Although the terrorists managed to kill and maim thousands of people, their families, and friends, this will not keep our nation in a state of fear. We are free and will remain free for all time.

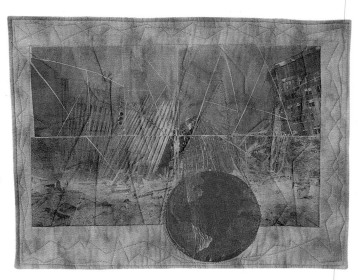

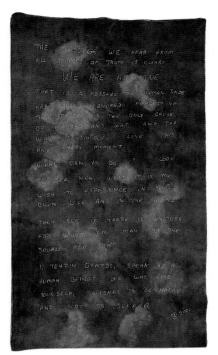

Hell at Zero / Hope at Zero

18" x 30" Mary Stevens
Waverly, AL USA

In the week following September 11, 2001, I felt sad, disconnected and unable to concentrate…While sorting through my hand dyes, I found this piece. The colors and patterns suggested terror and fire; another section seemed more peaceful. The top, Hell at Zero, *represents the horror of bombing, burning, death, and fear. This is pain and loss. The lower piece,* Hope at Zero, *represents the hope for recovery, the strength of the rescue workers and the residents, and the freeing of the spirits of the victims. This is release and growth.*

How Did It All Go Wrong?

16" x 28½" Thelma Smith
Green Valley, AZ USA

I had been reading Ethics for the New Millennium *by the Dalai Lama. The words were soft and gentle. The whole tenor of the book exuded serenity, plain common sense, and goodness. And then the towers came down. I had turned on the TV to check on the weather for a friend… Shock followed shock and sadness compounded. I firmly believe that each and every human acts from good intent. I also know that good intent can become twisted into horrible things. I know that even fanatics have ethical systems and that they expect good to come from their actions. It was hard to remember that teaching. It is still difficult to understand how we can go so wrong. I give you the words of His Holiness, the Dalai Lama.*

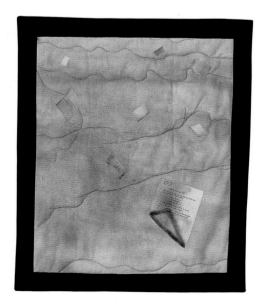

Out of a Clear Blue Sky

40" x 20" Caitlin O'Connor Toohey
Canberra ACT, Australia

This small, simple quilt was based on a news report about an Australian living in New Jersey discovering pieces of paper from offices in the World Trade Center buildings fluttering to the ground in her yard on the morning of September 11—the first she knew of the terrorist attack.

Those thousands of pieces of paper falling out of the blue, blue sky became for me an image representing the moment of change, an instant which divided our lives into before, and after.

PALE HORSE

17" x 16" Maxine Farkas
Lowell, MA USA

Pale horse
wanders
confused
abandoned
its harsh master
using different transport
this new millennium.

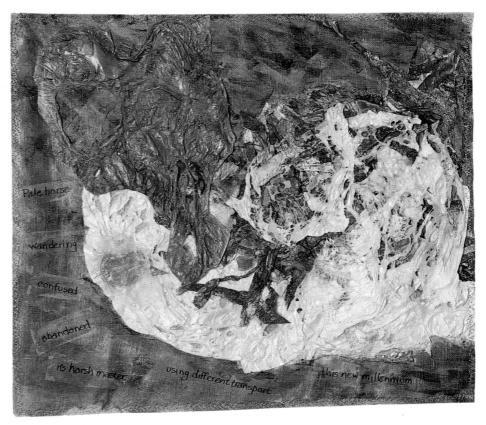

TO BE NOT AFRAID—
A REMEMBRANCE
OF THE DAY OF SADNESS

42" x 34" Claudia Comay
Oakland, CA USA

On September 11, 2001 I woke up to the measured tone of National Public Radio's Bob Edwards' voice and instantly knew that something terrible had happened... I watched and watched transfixed and for the next two weeks had a hard time functioning well.

I had never felt so vulnerable, so fearful, so angry, so fragile. I found myself unable to work. Unable to concentrate, I walked around with my heart clutched in my hands and my eyes blinded by tears...Two and a half weeks later, I slowly realized that life, imperfect and unfair as it is, goes on. I became defiant and I poured my soul back into my art. I had regained my purpose... Resilient and indomitable, I will not give up my hope and optimism to fear.

REACHING UP TO THE SKY

22" x 22½" Elizabeth Rosenberg
Yorktown Heights, NY USA

As an American, I was horrified when I saw the images of the two hijacked planes crashing into the Twin Towers. As a native New Yorker who has lived and worked in the shadow of those beautiful buildings, I felt the attack was personal.

As a quilter, I needed to make a quilt that would be a tribute …expressing how proud I am to be a New Yorker. I tried to make a quilt that showed how much the World Trade Center symbolized the strength and grandeur of New York City…

PRAY FOR NEW YORK

19" x 31" Janet Ghio
Columbia, MO USA

The events of September 11, 2001 shocked all of us…

The images of the World Trade Center were etched in my mind and I needed to visually express the sadness, grief and shock I was feeling, but also hope for tomorrow.

The design of the buildings came together pretty quickly. I wanted the devastation and the rubble to show through the inside-out seams and the threads hanging off. I left the edges of the quilt raw, just as I was feeling raw around the edges. Adding Our Lady of Guadalupe in the sky above New York was comforting. She represents compassion, love, and healing and is surrounded by angels quilted into the background…

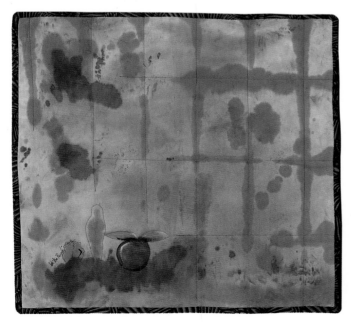

FROM THE ASHES OF HATRED, LOVE WILL PREVAIL

20½" x 20½" Carolyn Hoots Johnson
Germantown, TN USA

"WE THE PEOPLE" —that's who we are, the people, and we will emerge from the ashes and not be defeated. This is a time when everyone should lean on each other. Together we will be stronger than ever. We can be normal in a world gone mad.

In Memoriam

20" x 26" Joanie San Chirico
Toms River, NJ USA

I took this picture in February 2001 after a wonderful birthday spent with my daughter who lives in New York City. It was a cold, crisp winter day and the sun was setting creating beautiful patterns on the World Trade Center. A New York City sunset will never be the same, the world has now changed, my photograph is now obscured. My quilt, In Memoriam *is a tribute to those families who lost loved ones in these senseless attacks.*

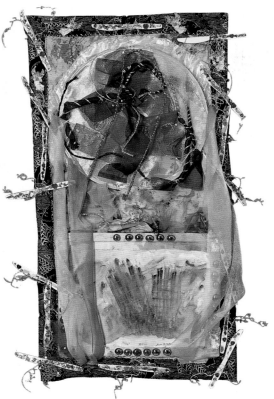

Rise

18" x 36" Susan McMillen
Wooster, OH USA

September 11, 2001 was the bleakest day I can recall… the dull gray smoke and ash that covered everything after the Trade Center collapsed, as though life no longer existed in chromatic colors. It was as if the terrorists socked the rainbow right in the solar plexus…I was inspired to paint in watercolor but the images of the tragedy continued to haunt me. I began this quilt to give myself something to do, I had already donated blood, contributed money, called my family and friends to tell them I love them…but it just didn't feel like that was enough…I hope that the women and the orphaned children will be protected for the rest of their lives from the atrocities, hatred, and fear of the Taliban.

One Life Lost - 6000 Times

35" x 26" Gerry Macsai
Evanston, IL USA

…As I tried to grasp the enormity of this horrible tragedy, I could only think of how each person was lost to people who loved him or her. The children, parents, lovers, wives and husbands, cousins, classmates, exercise buddies, hang-out buddies, best friends…all the rings of loss. There is no way to go back to normal, to go on with life. All we can do is try to patch together a new way to get through each day and patch together our lives. I wanted to emphasize the reality of each life because they should never be forgotten by the world…The transformation of the rubble into trees is an attempt to project the need we all have to find some way to live in the future.

These Colors Don't Run

We as a nation must never forget!

RESOLUTE, 30¾" x 38¼", **Caryl Gaubatz,** New Braunfels, TX USA

I wanted to concentrate on something positive—the triumph of the American spirit. I chose American symbols; the American bald eagle, and the flag. We are together in this. We are united. We are resolute.

THE WORLD WE KNEW

19" x 23" Lois Laird
Branson, MO USA

This was a spontaneous, impromptu reaction to the events of September 11th. I depicted New York City, our nation's capital, and the American flag made from various materials I have used in the past. I hope to illustrate the pride that I feel as an American and cause the viewer to reflect on the privileges that we enjoy as American citizens.

AMERICAN LIBERTY

34" x 27" Rebecca Nelson-Zerfas
Beulah, MI USA

After viewing so many depressing photos, I saw one that had the Statue of Liberty in the background. It reminded me of what she has stood for to so many people: the hopes and dreams that in this country they and future generations will find a better life.

A TIME TO REFLECT
37" x 30" Rita Micek
Duncan, NE USA

When I heard about the tragedies on 9/11/01, I was deeply saddened at the many lives lost and the injuries sustained, so when designing this quilt I wanted to include the different symbols, which I feel represent our country. I first thought of the flag and how it represents our free country. To make the stripes for the flag, I selected different fabrics to represent the many nationalities that live in our nation. The four people represent the four airplanes and many lives that were destroyed in the attack. I made them to hold hands representing the unity of our country. The skyline was added to remind us of New York City. From there, I felt I needed to design the tumbled frames of the World Trade Towers and the rubbish surrounding it as well as the smoke and dust rising from them. I thought the upper right corner was a perfect place to set the partial Statue of Liberty crown and the United We Stand slogan.

We need to be what we always have been—free.

SEPTEMBER II, 2001
53½" x 28½" Patty Gamburg
Alexandria, LA USA

I have used the gold crosses covering the towers to represent the loss of so many innocent lives.

The words on the center panel depict my reaction to and the range of emotions evoked by the terrorist attack. I hope someday to add the word forgiveness to the list. The flag is a reminder of the precious freedom I enjoy every day.

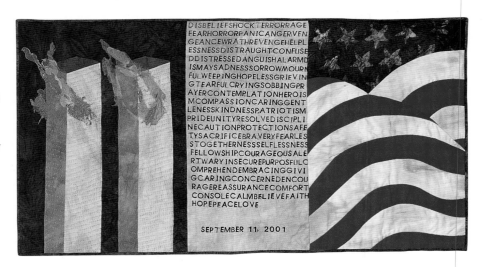

WE WILL REMEMBER

22½" x 36½" Ginger Burris
Coral Springs, FL USA

*The morning of September 11th I went into my
sewing room, turned on the television and began
to get ready to sew. One of the World Trade Center
buildings was smoking and on fire. The announcer
was trying to explain what was happening, as
another plane crashed into the second building.
At that moment I saw our world change. How
could this happen? We will remember the attack.
We will remember the victims. We must
remember how life was before, and hopefully
can be again. God Bless America.*

UNITED, WE'LL STAND

25" x 24" Ann H. Jones
Nevada, MO USA

*This is a simple quilt from the heart. From the
subtle quilting of the states, to the flag proudly
protecting them, we the people will stand as
one behind what we believe in and protect it.
No matter our religious or political difference,
our regional or social upbringing. With a pride
so fierce, a determination so strong, and a unity
so bonded that no one will be able to break it.*

*As I pieced this quilt, I realized that as one person,
I couldn't make much of a difference in what
happens. But, if we work as one nation against
a common evil, we will defend what we believe
in, what the founding fathers and those after
them fought for, and what we want for future
generations—a country that is free.*

PATCHES OF FREEDOM

48" x 38" Darlene Rengler
Port Aransas, TX USA

Working on this quilt for the last few weeks has helped me with the horrors of 9/11. Uncle Sam, The Last Alarm and Ground Zero are all back dropped by a collection of patches representing Americana and flags of the other countries.

WE WILL NEVER FORGET

36" x 28" Mary Barnett
Richmond, VA USA

I wanted to create a quilt that would capture many of the feelings associated with the terrorist attacks of September 11, 2001: shock, horror, fear, anger, patriotism, sadness, sympathy, resolve and an over-whelming feeling of disbelief.

I was at an out-of-state conference the day of the attacks…It seemed right to create a quilt with input, from different areas of the country, and as I looked at headlines in newspapers that my family had saved for me while I was away, I realized that this was the answer. Headlines from newspapers from all over the USA…are represented here.

As I researched headlines I discovered that there was little variance from state to state; I guess no matter where we live the emotions this horrible attack engendered are much the same. The Twin Towers were part of my initial design, but it took my son to remind me to add the Pentagon. Heroes in New York, Pennsylvania, and at the Pentagon are represented, as well, and the backing has a red cross on it, a tribute to all the organizations and individuals who provided aid and comfort.

GOD BLESS AMERICA

81" x 52" Sandy Crawford
Boulder City, NV USA

A brand new Veteran's Home (Nevada Veterans Nursing Home) is being built in Boulder City. Our quilt group made this quilt to give to them. It will be hung in one of the visiting areas. Since God Bless America has become our unofficial national anthem, we quilted those words into our flag. We wanted it to be subtle. You won't see the words in photographs. You have to be close to the flag to appreciate what it means to us. On November 11, 2001, Veteran's Day, the NVNH held a Flag Presentation and Dedication Ceremony on the premises. Everyone in our group got to be a part of the celebration. Our veterans mean so much to us. God bless and protect all involved in this new war.

OUT OF THE RUBBLE

36" x 36" Lonnie Schlough
Woodlands, TX USA

*"...send these, the homeless, tempest-tost to me... your huddled masses yearning to breathe free..."
These words are from* The New Colossus, *a poem written by Emma Lazarus in 1883. A bronze plaque of this poem sits at the base of the Statue of Liberty. Thank you, Peter Max, for inspiration.*

In Strength and Unity

12½" x 9" Diane Becka
North Bend, WA USA

That day I sat in shock, scared, crying for those who might be hurt and injured. Praying that it might be a nightmare, realizing it was not, and still, not believing. In the aftermath, what I saw gave me hope. People came together to help each other and stand as one. The flags were everywhere. As I drove across the west, I was moved by the strength and courage of the people, displaying the colors that symbolize the strength of the nation and make us united.

Dark Day for America

30" x 30" Betty Frezon
Rensselaer, NY USA

On September 11, 2001 we were entertaining family and friends at Brant Lake, NY. It was a beautiful day full of promise. At a little before 9 A.M., the phone rang. It was our son, Michael, with news about the first tower and while we spoke, the second plane struck. He is a newsperson and knew it was terrorists. He called many times keeping us informed… We all felt a loss and sadness in the pit of the stomach, which will linger for a long time. The square I used in my quilt is an old one entitled New York. In two blocks I used the traditional block. In the others I used the 2000 fabric that showed many famous landmarks in the USA. I did not find one for Pennsylvania but my thoughts and prayers are there with those heroes and their families. I hope doing this quilt helps me and others who see it start to heal.

AMERICAN HEART

47" x 47" Jean Kaste
Fort Wayne, IN USA

September 11, 2001 has become a day that people all over the world will never forget. As I watched on television the horror of the events unfold, my heart and soul cried. Too many people hurt, too many people lost, and too much evil. All of our hearts were touched, and this quilt is meant to represent just that. As days followed, I soon learned how caring the rest of the world was…People everywhere shared the pain of that day, and by taking some of the grief, they eased ours. Our hearts were touched, just as I am sure your heart is being touched by viewing this wonderful exhibit. Thank you to those who worked so hard for giving all quilters a chance to show their love of the USA and their caring spirit.

MY GRAND OLD FLAG

42" x 27" Jo Ann Brown
Danbury, CT USA

I started this flag on September 14, 2001, three days after the terrorism perpetrated on the World Trade Center and Pentagon, and completed it on September 28, 2001. The design is an original by Jackie Robinson called Long May She Wave.

As I walked around the Pennsylvania National Quilt Expo on Thursday, September 13, 2001 seeing empty booths, classes cancelled, black ribbons, and feeling a somber atmosphere, this pattern which is sold on my website—came to mind. The more I thought about it, the more determined I was to take some action of my own in retaliation.

The action of creating a patriotic symbol started the healing process within me.

GOD BLESS AMERICA

26" x 18" Martha Burt White
Wheaton, MD USA

After listening to the news for four hours on the morning of September 11, 2001, I immediately went and hung my American flag on my front porch. I also wanted a small flag to hang on my mantle—I did not have one. That was when this wallhanging began. I found a pattern from a book and went into my stash, just looking for red, white, and blue fabric. I found many pieces of those three colors containing stars. Just as I was getting ready to put the fabric away, I noticed the blue piece of fabric with the United States Capitol on it. It was at that moment that a chill went down my back as I remembered that that piece of fabric also had included the skyline of New York City. I found that piece and knew at once that I should make more than just a flag. I collected more fabric, buttons, and ribbon and set to work. Making this wallhanging really helped me get through that awful day and remember how proud I was to be able to say "I am proud to be an American!"

SHAKEN, BUT NOT BROKEN

39" x 36" Karen Sue Whiteside
Marion, Ohio USA

*September 11, 2001 will be a day that will forever be imprinted in my brain...But when the scenes started showing thousands of people running for their very lives from the heavy clouds of smoke and debris, it hit me that this was no movie I was watching. My shock turned to a steady stream of tears...numb with shock, grief and horror that this could be happening to our country...That was when I decided I had to do something...I proceeded to make quilts for the young children that lost their brave parents, praying fervently for their families the whole time. I then decided that I also needed a quilt to express my rage, grief, and sorrow over these horrific events...
The stars that surround my quilt were made to reflect that very feeling that I felt. As President Bush said, "We have been shaken, but not broken."...I am so proud of our country and how it has united together again to become a nation under God. GOD BLESS AMERICA!
In memory of Chuck Jones, Bob Penninger, and Gerard Moran, employees of Bae Systems, Inc.*

E Pluribus Unum:
Courage and Tolerance

60" x 40" Susi Soler
Valrico, FL USA

I began this quilt in August, 2001, because of a local incident. An ignorant woman went to my local librarian and told her she should, "go back where you came from!" My librarian, a kind, gentle, woman named Xianai Mi, just ignored her, but she was very hurt. Me, I was livid!

Xianai is from China and she is an American citizen…When I started this quilt, it was to honor Xianai, but I had intentions of keeping it for myself. After the attacks on America on 9/11/01, I knew I had to finish this quilt and put it in this exhibit, because I think a huge part of being an American is having courage and tolerance.

Xianai had a lot of courage, from being that little girl of 12, to have the goal to come to America. As the melting pot that America originated from, we Americans need to remember what our country was founded on, and spend a little time learning to be more tolerant of our fellow citizens. When the exhibit is over, the quilt is going to my friend, Xianai, to let her know that she is wanted in our country and I hope no one, ever again, tells her to "go back where you came from…."

Attack on America

49¾" x 56" Patricia Diaz
Lenore, ID USA

Like everyone else in the United States on September 11, 2001, I watched the television in growing disbelief, horror, sadness, and anger. Two days passed and then I felt the incredible need to create a quilt—to try and permanently record in fabric what happened that day—the day that changed our world. The quilt needed to be a memorial to all those who lost their lives at the terrorists' hands. My quilt guild had just started a "row of the month" project. This seemed like the perfect "pattern" to use since it was so difficult to think…the creating of it proved to be greatly cathartic. When I learned about AMERICA: From the Heart, I hurried to finish the quilt so my voice could be heard, and perhaps my quilt would help in the healing process.

One Heart...One Nation

27" x 27" Susan Yonkers
Averill Park, NY USA

This quilt was made as a challenge piece for East Side Quilters, a quilt guild located in upstate New York. It was due on September 18, 2001. Our guild challenge was to make a quilt that was inspired by a song lyric, poem, story, et cetera, and contained at least one Nine-Patch or Nine-Patch variation block. One Heart...One Nation...I chose the song God Bless America as my inspiration, and only a day or two before our Open House, started piecing and sewing my quilt top...

As the media coverage of these tragic events filled our minds with horror and destruction and unnecessary loss of lives, I was touched by the outpouring of love and togetherness from so many...people of all religions and nationalities in cities and towns across our great nation and around the world, granted us solace for those lost and time to reflect and pray in unity for peace, understanding and compassion. I was also heartened by the display of American flags flying everywhere you looked, as a great tribute to our loyalty and patriotism and freedom that cannot be taken away. God Bless America!

Mending American Hearts

16" x 20" Steph Winn
Las Vegas, NV USA

I sat up tonight making this quilt watching the news and crying, feeling lonely except for the things and the people I see. I see people in NY and everywhere I look come together, I see them behaving the way I want my children to be, being strong and brave, fighting for what is right. I see them fighting back the tears of fear and trusting our government to do the right thing. I see people at a baseball game crying when they sing the National Anthem feeling the uncertainty and fear of what's been happening. I see a strong news anchorman break down on a show, being human. I see people coming together. I feel like this horrible thing has brought people together like nothing could have. In tragedy people come together... Everyone wishes they could mend the hearts of the families and friends of the victims. To stand strong and help support the things our country and the world is going through, and will go through...I always want to fix things, but I can't fix this...So I sat and mended American hearts. God Bless America.

THEY HURT OUR HEARTS

28" x 36" Susan Stidman Lewis
Arvada, CO USA

The words of 10-year-old Hillary McLean from Denver that she wrote to the firefighters in New York City sum up my quilt: "They hurt our hearts, but our spirit still flies." I wanted this quilt to show our pain and grief in these tattered and frayed hearts.

The waving red and white stripes symbolize our unity in displaying "Old Glory."…The eagle flies high at the top showing pride and freedom. The foundation-pieced eagle is taken from, Paper Piecing the Seasons by Liz Schwartz and Stephen Seifert. The national bird has an olive branch for peace on one side, and an arrow symbolizing strength on the other side.

The stars on the quilt border represent the commitment and support of the firefighters, rescue workers and relief workers. Their work and sacrifice binds us together. Good overcomes evil and love conquers hate. We are united in our grief and strong in our faith. Forever changed, we can gain by coming together and striving to keep our spirit soaring!

IT WAS THE WORST OF TIMES

31" x 25½" Mace B. McEligot
Manasquan, NJ USA

September 11, 2001, was a beautiful day until 8:43 A.M. I could not believe what I was seeing and found myself waiting for "the other shoe to drop." I needed an activity to get my mind off of the horror of this tragedy, so I started dyeing fabric for a quilt that would be a tribute to those lives that were lost. My quilt shows the attempt by the attackers to shatter our country and our way of life, our broken hearts for the victims and their families. The bunting and the badges are a tribute to all of the emergency workers, and the flag under it shows that our country will recover, but we will never forget these terrible deeds!

MY TEARS OF LOST INNOCENCE

100" x 92" Donnely Lockard
Spring Lake, MI USA

I was reading my morning email on 9/11/2001, when I heard 3-year-old Raven say, "plane broke it." Thinking he had broken something, I went to the living room. Seeing nothing I glanced at the TV, they were showing the plane hitting the towers, over, and over again. Sinking to the floor with Raven on my lap, all I could do was cry and say, "What have they done?" As the morning went on, there was more destruction. It was overwhelming. I couldn't stop the tears, one family was safe, but not the rest...

Like so many other quilters and artists, I needed to create something to help ease the pain, to have something to remember that day. Taking two days to create my eagle, I then designed around him. There was much I wanted to include, but so little space. The stars symbolized all the nations that lost people, the colors are from past war-time eras. The world with doves a hope of world peace...

SPIRIT OF AMERICA

40½" x 29½" Christy Johnston
Houston, TX USA

"For this is what America is all about. It is the uncrossed desert and the unclimbed ridge. It is the star that is not reached and the harvest that is sleeping in the unplowed ground." —Lyndon Baines Johnson, Presidential inaugural address (Jan. 20, 1965).

In 1782, the Second Continental Congress declared the bald eagle the official National Emblem of the United States. As a part of the seal of the United States of America, the eagle holds a banner that says E pluribus unum*–"Out of Many, One." Just as this quilt is one image made of many pieces, so our country is one nation made of many individuals, our world made of many nations.*

Spirit of America was made to remember the victims of September 11, 2001, to honor the rescue workers and members of the armed services who risked and gave their lives, and to inspire all of us to live our lives reaching for the stars.

No Fear

40" x 28" Jane A. Damico
Houston, TX USA

Since September 11, along with the rest of the nation, I had been going through the process of feeling shock, disbelief, anger and finally a deep grief for the families in the World Trade Center. It was not until I heard these words, "The bald eagle was chosen as a symbol for America because it is not afraid to fly into a storm" that I began to feel inspired and energized.

My hope for America is that we will not be afraid of this storm of terrorism, that we rebuild...that we defend our freedom that is now more precious than ever before.

...I was sparked by the rich traditional art works produced by a needle, some thread and an array of fiber and textile that is deeply rooted in the feminine world. Formed by a variety of techniques and inspired by the landscape of the land, my works embody my Mexican-American blood...

Land That I Love

27" x 27" Cynthia England
Houston, TX USA

WRAPPED IN GLORY

40" x 32½" Judy Zoelzer Levine
Bayside, WI USA

Patriotic, counted, proud. The flag is wrapped around the image of a female torso. When we speak of freedom, we speak about protecting our hearth and home. Females usually represent Liberty and justice. But the flag around the female image also represents the freedoms women enjoy in our country; the freedom to pursue careers, education, and fulfilling lives. We also enjoy full and equal protection under the law.

LET FREEDOM RING

42" x 42" Alison Dale
Evergreen, CO USA

There are images of September 11th that speak to all Americans; the images I have chosen speak specifically to me. I've lived in New York and Washington. The Twin Towers will always remain a memory of my time in New York, and I could see the Washington Monument from my apartment window. I have lived in the suburbs of both New York City and Washington, D.C. It was hard to see the cities endure so much horror. I have competed in two Marine Corps Marathons in Washington. I will never forget the people who supported the runners. My best wishes to the people of New York and Washington.

SOLIDARITY

16" x 16" Debbie Markowitz
Jerusalem, Israel

"Everything that happens here, it's all a miracle, and nothing happens for no reason, and God knows what he's doing. He wants to tell us that we need to behave better, and that soon the Messiah will come, and that then all the dead will rise again." –Chaya Schijveschuurder, age 8, who was seriously injured, along with her sister, and lost both parents and three siblings, in the suicide bombing of the Sbarro restaurant in Jerusalem.

*In memory of cousin Nancy Morgenstern, lost in the WTC.
In honor of ALL victims of ALL terrorism ALL over the world.*

MENDING OF THE HEART

14½" x 18" Sandra Wagner
Pine Grove, CA USA

There are so many hearts that have been affected by the tragedy of September 11, 2001, and as a nation we will be mending hearts for many years to come.

My feelings for this quilt are represented by the torn fabric strips that show the lives that have been torn apart. The black netting represents the black smoke that hangs over the sites; the broken heart is for the ones left behind; the burned heart is for the lives lost; and the American bald eagle is holding the heart that is mending a nation.

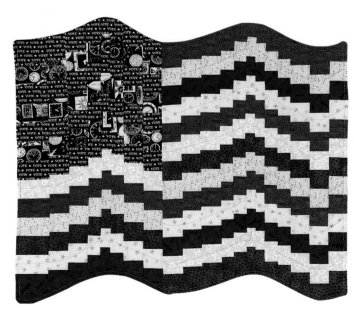

IT'S TIME FOR OLD GLORY

25" x 22" Cynthia Pierron Janney
Fernandina Beach, FL USA

*It's time for Old Glory to wave!
Time for all of us to reflect upon our flag!
Time to unite under her proud banner.
Old Glory reflects all that is good with America.
She waves for freedom!
May God bless her and may ever she wave!*

WE SHALL NOT FORGET

53" x 42" Sue Vanderveen
Ramona, CA USA

*On September 11, 2001, three employees of
Bae Systems, Inc., the company I've worked for
the past 23 years, lost their lives to terrorist
activity. One was on the plane that struck the
second World Trade Center building, one was
on the plane that struck the Pentagon and the
third was in the Pentagon. This quilt was made
in their memory and to the thousands who lost
their lives that day and to the loved ones left
behind...The quotes penned in the white stripes
are from great Americans during difficult times
such as these...*

E PLURIBUS UNITY

16" x 13" Karen A. Neary
Amherst, Nova Scotia Canada

*The title of this little quilt tailors the motto of the
United States e pluribus Unum to reflect the
world's response to the terrorist attacks of
September 11, 2001.*

*Geographically and historically, Canada and the
United States have always been close. Many of our
sons and daughters died in this attack. We join with
countries around the world in pledging our support
against terrorism.*

*In e pluribus Unity the flags of our countries are
arranged to form a heart; the Rising Sun block
peeking up behind the two flags is quilted with a
thread (YLI "Glowbug") which glows in the dark.
Even when things seem dark, unity from many gives
strength and hope for better tomorrows.*

GOD BLESS AMERICA

12" x 12" Donna Robinson
Anaheim, CA USA

The American flag represents it all to me. I felt absolutely compelled to make a block of our flag. My tears have not stopped...God Bless America.

FRACTURED FLAG

37" x 32" Diane M. Kammlah and Rose Wilson
Fredricksburg, TX USA

Rose and I designed this flag a year ago because we both love patriotic designs. We felt that after the tragedy of 9/11 we had to do something. Working on this project has been difficult. One of the most moving photos from New York was the picture of the firemen raising our flag in the rubble of the World Trade Center. It gave us hope that even though this horrible event had occurred, our country was still strong and so was its symbol. The flag is at half-mast to honor those that died, but the sentiment is based on our basic beliefs—that we are proud to be Americans and we cherish our freedoms.

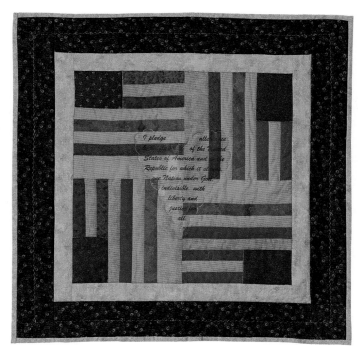

MY PLEDGE

27" x 27" Sandy Rogers
Covina, CA USA

I was fortunate to have traveled with the late (and great) Doreen Speckmann on several quilt tours to different parts of the world. We met the most delightful people with friendly smiles and warm hearts in each of the countries. Quilters speak a language unique to their craft and straight from the heart. We as quilters have an opportunity to share not only the warmth that is a by-product of our skills, but our feelings for the human race. I suggest we make two quilts: one for a family of an American lost on September 11th, the other with a pieced or appliqued heart, to be sent to Afghanistan.

LAND THAT I LOVE
22" x 17" Betty Alofs
Lakeside, CA USA

As I thought about recent events, I wondered in awe at the strength of character, the dedication, the willing sacrifices made by Americans helping America. I thought of all the things I love about this country and I felt pride to see the American flag boldly displayed at homes, in the workplace, on cars and trucks, on lapels—everywhere. We were united...The phrases of the Pledge of Allegiance, God Bless America and the Star Spangled Banner all intermingling...came to mind. These words are heartfelt, as is the love for our country and grief for our great losses. Our very values are at stake, and we once again muster all the strength we have been given by being Americans. We the people of the United States of America...stand united still.

Very touching to see all those across the world who care.

AMERICA AWAKENS
22½" x 12" Clara Lawrence
Elgin, TX USA

About the quilt: this happens to be my second finished quilt, of course I have another five in process. I had a thought the day of September 11th that patriotism was to be a part of our lives and for a lot of us, including myself, for the first time...

The morning after, I sent out an Email to everyone I knew and all major networks and the New York Daily News. It went like this...

Tomorrow Starts Today. Tomorrow has come today and all is different and will never be the same. This haunts me as I look upon my two little ones, and wonder what the future will be like for them... If there is any good it will come from unity. Patriotism will be a new thing for so many Americans. I welcome it today. Priorities can be wrapped up clearly in three categories...Family, friends, and country. Everything else seems petty and will hopefully remain there today...To all those I write this to...I send my love and hopes for the future for all the children.

MOURN WITH THOSE WHO MOURN

48" x 32" Jennilyn Landbeck
Forest Hill, MD USA

The title of this quilt comes from the scriptures. (Mosiah 18:9, The Book of Mormon, Another Testament of Christ) I couldn't stop watching the news stories: the prayers and hopes, the phone calls, the good-byes of "I love you!…"

A quilter quilts. I pulled out my box of stashed patriotic fabrics, things I had been gathering for years for a someday "Americana" quilt…I was sad, and made a sad flag. But there are hopeful, united, patriotic sections in the stripes. I felt numbered among the mourning and ever hopeful for peace… "all those who have mourned shall be comforted…for all flesh is in mine hands; be still and know that I am God" —Doctrine & Covenants 101:14,16

NEVER FORGET

25" x 35" Amanda Schlatre
Houston, TX USA

For me, the statement that stuck, after the events of September 11 was from the Star Spangled Banner: "…land of the free and home of the brave." I wanted my quilt to reflect the enduring spirit and patriotic fervor of the country…I wanted my quilt to say, "Do not forget the thousands who were taken from us on 9.11…by upholding the vision for which our country stands—tolerance, freedom, equal rights, opportunity…"

GAIL'S PEACE DOVES

36" x 45" Shari Adkisson
Houston, TX USA

In response to the tragedy of September 11, 2001, this quilt is inspired by a quote from my Minister, Gail Lindsay-Marriner of First Unitarian Universalist Church. Her quote is, "In my spare moments I'm trying to figure out how to morph stars into doves so I can create a flag where the stars in the field of blue transform into birds of peace as you scan from left to right." As I read Gail's comments, I could "see" this quilt in my mind…The peace doves are taken from a children's website, Peace Pals, and are created from fabric applied to freezer paper.

LIBERTY WATCHES THE WRATH OF MAN

27" x 47" Elizabeth Spilker
Westerville, OH USA

In this piece, Liberty watches as men's anger consumes others. If we turned our backs to the destruction and viewed Liberty from the other side, what would we see? If we viewed Liberty from God's perspective, what would we learn?

Like many Americans on September 11, 2001, I watched in disbelief as our nation was attacked. I stood alone in my home and sang A Mighty Fortress is Our God. I was reminded that my security does not come from buildings, wealth, or governments. It lies in the name of the Lord. "The name of the Lord is a strong tower. The righteous runs into it and is safe." (Proverbs 16:10)

Like most Americans since that day, I have grieved the losses, but I have hope. "But we do not want you to be uninformed, brethren, about those who have fallen asleep, that you may not grieve, as do the rest who have no hope. For if we believe that Jesus died and rose again, even so God will bring with Him those who have fallen asleep in Jesus." (1 Thessalonians 4:13-14) "For God has not destined us for wrath, but for obtaining salvation through our Lord Jesus Christ, who died for us, that whether we are awake or asleep, we may live together with Him." (1 Thessalonians 5:9-10) "For the wrath of man does not achieve the righteousness of God." (James 1:20) "For God did not send the Son into the world to judge the world, but that the world should be saved through Him". (John 3:17)

MADE USA 2001

**24" x 23" Mary Mashuta and
Roberta Horton**
Berkeley, CA USA

This quilt represents the first joint quilt created by sisters Roberta Horton and Mary Mashuta even though each has been a quilter for over thirty years. Mary filled her original shirt block pattern with patriotic fabrics she began collecting during the Bicentennial. Roberta added a border that includes the words "Made USA". This is short for things associated with the United States such as: freedom, liberty, and the holding of individual opinions and beliefs.

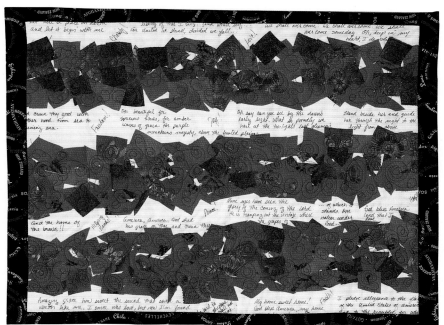

We Shall Overcome

24" x 19" Lynda Poole Prioleau
Fort Washington, MD USA

After the bombings, I found myself in a terrible state of shock. During the days that followed, I caught myself singing old hymns that I learned as a little girl. While watching various television programs, I noticed that music was a constant—the patriotic as well as the sacred.

In an effort to bring my feelings to fabric, I wrote some of the verses that brought calm to my heart. I included blocks of various red fabrics that represent the bloodshed of so many people. The white represents the hope and peace that I pray will never diminish. The blue border contains the names of many countries which, I hope, will learn to be more tolerant of each other so that this kind of tragedy will never happen again.

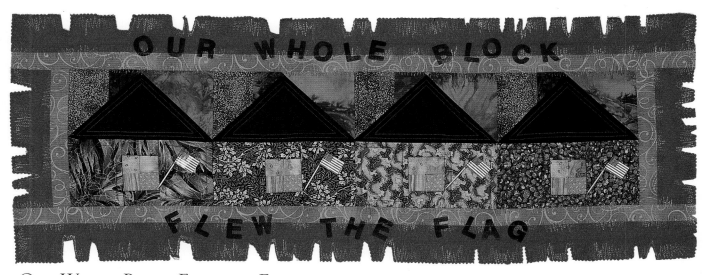

Our Whole Block Flew the Flag

37¼" x 14" Donna Mikesch
Kingwood, TX USA

Shortly after the terrible tragedies of September 11th, we put our flag out in response to all the patriotic activities. Soon I noticed that every house on our short block was proudly flying our flag. Perhaps one of the good things to come out of these horrible days is a return to patriotic feelings about our country. It is a great privilege to live in a country where we are free to practice our religion, to speak out as we see fit, to pursue jobs and activities we wish to and, as women, to be able to do all of the above. In spite of all its faults, we live in a remarkable country. We owe it to all of the people who lost their lives to keep it free. This quilt is made in response to all of this—the sadness, the courage, and patriotism.

UNITY

75½" x 97" Becky Marshall
Murfreesboro, TN USA

MOURNING

64" x 64" Mona Clark
Rochester, NH USA

Tuesday, September 11, 2001. Who in the whole world will ever forget this date? On that date, I was on my way to attend the "Pennsylvania Quilt Extravaganza" in Fort Washington, PA. About twenty miles from New York City we suddenly saw blinking lights on the highway stating that "ALL NYC BRIDGES CLOSED. SEEK ALTERNATE ROUTE." We immediately turned on the car radio and I honestly thought that I was listening to a TV or movie ad...When we checked into our room we immediately turned on the TV, and everything that we had imagined while traveling was so much less than what we were seeing. We just sat there in shock...From the time we arrived home we had the TV set on MSNBC permanently... I am still hoping and praying for all the families to find peace and closure for their loved ones. Please Lord, watch over us all and keep us safe.

THE DAY THE EAGLE CRIED

23" x 19" Janell Gust
Claycomo, MO USA

As my husband and I were in North Dakota with family, preparing to come back to Missouri, my heart sank...Through the many miles of driving there were many things that crossed in my mind. #1 was that my family would all be okay when I reached home. #2 As an EMS worker in Kansas City, I thought of the tragedy of our Union brothers and sisters in the EMS, police and firefighter fields...many would not be making it home to their families...

My children talked about it daily. In weeks to come a 9/11 wall quilt was started to ease some of the fears. Everyone from my husband to the youngest child, along with a few friends, had input in the quilt. A special thanks to Sharyn Riggs, who did the machine quilting. The crying eagle is how many of us felt that day. But leave it to Old Glory to shine through the 911...

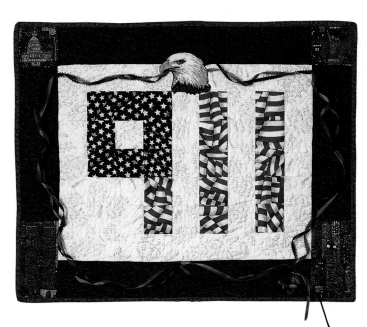

GODDESS OF AMERICA

30" x 39" Julie Stiller
Boulder Creek, CA USA

The Goddess of America rises up from the dark, stormy, confusing skies swirling about the shining cities of our country. She is the Anno Domini—Lady of Abundance. She reminds us that all the bounty of this country is here for all members of our society…She sternly and seriously asks us to consider how we use these gifts she has given us…And finally she asks us as a people to try to work through the stages of anger, hostility, fear, and despair to come to the point of compassion for the attackers. Not forgiveness, but compassion for these men that had nothing else but their hatred of our country to sustain and motivate them.

JOURNAL ENTRY UNNUMBERED

27" x 37" Linda Baker
Lake Oswego, OR USA

Unnumbered has a double meaning: 1) Not countable; too many to count; 2) Lacking identifying number; not assigned or having an identified number. (Encarta World English Dictionary).

Working through my feelings about the September 11th, 2001, attack on the Twin Towers and the Pentagon, I found myself journaling more in my mind than on paper. It seemed like a continuous, uncountable dialogue, much like the reality of war where there are days and days on end of battles being waged. I've never understood war as a solution, so this has been a deep struggle for me…I've experienced a new energy to give back to all of humanity from creating this piece. I am still searching for what justice really means, but this was one way to start.

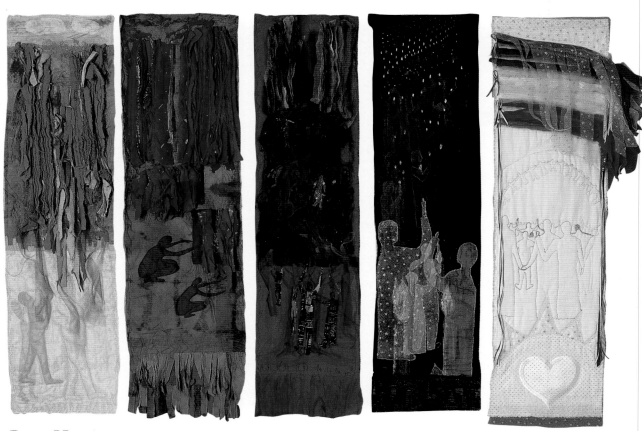

RAW...HOPE

75" x 56" Marlene Glickman
Clearwater, FL USA

Panel 1: "Raw Shock" Watching the towers and Pentagon on TV over and over again and hearing how many people were there when the planes crashed was more than I could take. I began to rip fabric in anger and sorrow for all those lost. I didn't want to plan or cut carefully, feeling raw with shock and disbelief.

Panel 2: "Searching" Immediately, the search for survivors began, looking in the rubble of the towers, the Pentagon and elsewhere, people looking in hospitals and the streets for loved ones hoping they had escaped with their lives.

Panel 3: "Saying Goodbye" to those we know are physically gone. Hoping they left their bodies and buildings quickly and are looking down seeing those who love them handle the loss. Hoping they will be able to do something to ease the pain.

Panel 4: "Gathering Together" The memorial service, with others, candles burning in memory of those who gave their lives, unexpectedly; flags waving; honoring those lost and those still with us. Each person carries a light to heal the personal hurt, shock, and wounds of the nation.

Panel 5: "Uniting in Hope" How to go from the hurt to hope for a different future, one in which we can all make changes. Americans remember its pledge to ensure hope and freedom from oppression. Each person can make a difference, can change things. You can help. Find out how.

AMERICA 911

80" x 90" Carol Thompson
Memphis, TN USA

Making this quilt was a source of comfort to me. I cried as I sewed, and at times my fingers cramped from holding the needle so tightly. But it helped me feel safe again. It will go on my bed to help me through the times ahead. In America 911 stars and stripes are dominant. Words such as "Resolve, Freedom, Honor, Oh Beautiful, God Bless, Peace, Land that I love, Home Sweet Home, United" that are written on this quilt express some values of my country that I hold dear.

THE BIRTHDAY GIFT

24" x 36" Brenda Edeskuty
Jemez Springs, NM USA

When my niece first learned the Pledge of Allegiance she very carefully wrote out the words, drew me a flag, and sent it to me for my birthday. I was so touched by her discovery of patriotism, love of the flag, and so tickled by the spelling that, I thought someday I would make a quilt. Seven years have passed but...I knew it was the right time for her beautiful expression of patriotism to come to life in a quilt. I will always have fond memories of my niece during her discovery of what it meant to be an American, and to date it is the most special "Birthday Gift" I have received.

OH! SAY CAN YOU SEE?

19" x 19" Patsy Monk
Parrish, FL USA

Roosters are up early in the morning, what better time to have looked for our "Stars and Stripes?..." They wake me early to greet the new day dawning. Many things about this piece remind me of the inner stability of our county. The background is a hand painted sky by Fabrics to Dye For. Ultra suede was used as it does not fray when stressed. The Red stripes looked like blood when painted. Silver metallic thread was quilted in sharp zigs and zags—reminding me of the many times our country has been involved in battles but has come out intact—whole...The shape is round, one symbol to remind me of GOD with never a beginning or an ending.

In GOD we still trust.

9/11 Heartache & Healing

47½" x 33¼" Wendy Ingham

Salt Lake City, UT USA

This quilt was made
To bring me peace
To heal the heartache
For those who have died

I sewed all Sunday
And twice through the night
I was driven by passion
And the hand of God

When I saw it complete
I began to cry
For this was the vision
Within my mind's eye

On the back is a message
God gave me the day
When we were all asked to stop
And at noon we would pray

I was then to place fabric
Of fire trucks and men
Who worked day and night
To save strangers and friends

Within the bricks
Are sprigs of green
This represents growth
And healing for all

Throughout the world
All hearts were joined
The stars are a symbol
Of brighter days

I release this quilt
To its perfect home
Through the power of prayer
We are never alone.

Uncle Sam—Through it All He Still Stands Tall

21½" x 56½" Jodi Spain

Stafford, TX USA

When I think about the tragedy of September 11th, it makes me incredibly proud to be an American. United we truly stood. Through all the pain, suffering, and wondering, Americans remained steadfast, proud, and unwavering. I felt that Uncle Sam was a good representation of us as Americans. Through it all, we still stand tall.

Damaged But Not Destroyed

23" x 24½" Sara Newberg King
Paducah, KY USA

I wept on September 11th. I imagine that most of the nation cried…After the initial sorrow, I prayed. I prayed for children who no longer could feel a loving hug from their father or mother. I prayed for parents who had lost a son or daughter. I prayed for President Bush and all world leaders who needed guidance in the days ahead. And I even prayed for Osama Bin Laden, who knows no love and therefore needs prayer the most…

Half Mast

23½" x 16½" Christina Hoyt
Colorado Springs, CO USA

Like everyone I was shocked by the destruction on Sept 11, 2001. I was moved by the spontaneous display of the American flag across the country and around the world. The world mourned with us. This quilt is meant to honor those who died and to help those left behind. I was frustrated that there wasn't more I could do that day but give blood. This is my donation to help those who suffer directly from this tragedy.

I pray for peace and hope that my 23-year-old son and his contemporaries will not die in war. Our generation may respond to this atrocity and send troops, but his generation will have to fight it. 911 still means help is on the way.

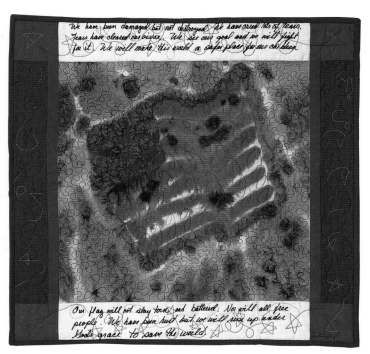

Impressions of a Tragedy

70" x 56" June Chinn
Vancouver, WA USA

This quilt was made to help me deal with the tragedy that started on September 11th and is still going on in our nation. Giving money and blood is helping our nation, but it doesn't take away the pain in my heart or the fear in my throat. This quilt is made up of the impressions of the horror that took place as well as the courageous steps that our nation has taken since September 11th. It is dedicated to the thousands of innocent people who lost their lives that day.

REMEMBER (ECCLESIASTES 9:11-12)

12" x 9" Patsy Monk
Parrish, FL USA

Remember *was brought to fiber following the events of 9/11/01. I began reading scripture for each 9:11 passage. Ecclesiastes 9:11 indicates life is not fair, just as it was not fair to the thousands upon thousands who lost lives, livelihoods and loved ones on that tragic day. Ecclesiastes 9:12 indicates that no man knows when the last day will occur. Scripture assisted my fearful and tearful days that followed…*

UNITY AMID TRAGEDY

35½" x 60" Barbara Drake
Spring Hill, FL USA

In making this quilt, I wanted to express how the USA has banded together after the tragedy of 9/11/01. The medallion in the center memorializes the lives lost in the World Trade Center, the Pentagon and United Flight 93. The eagle and Statue of Liberty were made 3D to look more lifelike as symbols of the fortitude of our glorious country.

SEPTEMBER 11, 2001

60" x 45" Judy Murrah
Victoria, TX USA

A few days before 9/11 I had pieced a quilt of simple 6½" squares with a single border that I intended to hand quilt and save for a future grandchild. When our nation was assaulted, my simple baby quilt top seemed trite. Instead, I slashed through the quilt the same way our calm existence had been abruptly disrupted. I added black strips of fabric to those slashed places to pull the quilt back together again…. I continued to add other mementos to the quilt to memorialize the lives that were so tragically lost to our nation in the attacks. The act of adding these things to my quilt was not unlike placing mementos on a grave. This was my statement: That the US would prevail, that those lives that were lost are now in heaven, and that they will not be forgotten by those of us who remain, to fight to hold our country together.

RIPPLES OF HOPE

15" x 25" Judy Fusco
Syracuse, NY USA

All of us are searching for meaning, for some way to put things together, for some way to move on… wondering if life will ever be the same…And as we work our way through all the questions and doubts and anger, because we are people of faith and action, we ask ourselves what can we DO?

ONE FOR ALL AND ALL FOR ONE

77" x 63" Natima Palaskas
New Zealander living in Abu Dhabi, United Arab Emirates

The reason for making this quilt was the shock I had seeing the events of September 11th unfold before my eyes on TV. I couldn't believe that it was happening. Even though I am not an American and not living in America, I have the same feeling of loss. Your loss is my loss, your safety is my safety. Quilters live in one world, the world of sharing, creating, making new friends and helping each other to make more quilts. As an expatriate and foreign resident, quilting has been my social anchor.

Special thanks to Donna Ward of New Zealand who did the machine quilting for me with such short notice.

A RED, WHITE & BLUE PRAYER

47½" x 39¾" Elizabeth Neimeyer
Houston, TX USA

This wallhanging was created as a gift for the DeGeorge Hotel, a shelter for homeless veterans in Houston. As they work to rebuild their lives, I wanted to remind them of the meaning of the colors that they fought for. After the tragedies of September 11th, I felt that these three words capsulated everything we were all praying for. God has granted us courage, remembrance and strength, may He continue to do so.

Stars and Stripes

13¾" x 12¾" Suzanne Riggio
Wauwatosa, WI USA

After the horrific events of September 11, 2001, I remembered, with a jolt, a piece of fabric by Fabric Traditions that I owned. It contained the New York skyline with the Twin Towers prominently shown. I had bought it to place in the heirloom quilt I am making for my son Paul, who lives in New York City with his wife Lynn and three children, Nalina, Zachary, and Sofia Rose. So when Karey Bresenhan in Houston announced the wall of impromptu quilts called "AMERICA: From the Heart" that would be shown this fall during Quilt Market and Quilt Festival, I knew I had to use this fabric. I cut out part of this skyline fabric, dulled the bright places with overlays, and shrouded the towers with white. Above them are ascending silver stars, representing the victims. The quilting is randomly vertical. The two shrouds, looking like stripes in our flag under those stars told me the name should be Stars and Stripes.

Fallout

39" x 13½" Leesa Zarinelli Gawlik
Hometown: Ste. Genevieve, MO
Hayama-machi Kanagawa, Japan

The title of my quilt was selected based on one definition of fallout: the incidental results or side effects. The glossy words at the bottom of my quilt are all taken from emotions immediately following the attacks. As they slowly drifted away, they were replaced with thoughts of how the events have changed us as individuals and as a nation. The use of lyrics from America the Beautiful reflects the empathy I feel for Muslim Americans, as well as other recent immigrants in their struggle to gain acceptance as loyal citizens of our country. The sky blue background fabric was dyed with fresh indigo from my garden. In Japan, indigo is believed to have a healing quality, which I experienced in the process of making this quilt.

Healing & Hope, Hearts on the Mend

The response of America has been what makes me proud to be an American.

MY HEART HURTS, **51" x 61" Margo Clyma,** Media, PA USA

My heart hurts from the anguish and pain, that so many have suffered from the September 11, 2001, attack on the United States. I am especially saddened for those families who must deal with the loss of their loved ones. How sad it is that we humans could be spending our time and talents to improve the lot of all human kind and yet we continue to hurt one another. Such a waste; it makes my heart hurt!

AMERICA'S TEARS

30" x 41" Linda Tunze Kennedy
Hazelwood, MO USA

We cried, in fear, in shock, in disbelief and anger. How could anyone hate us so much to take all of these innocent lives?

Our hearts were broken.

We cried as we heard their stories. Firemen, policemen, husbands, wives, mothers, fathers, children, lovers, friends— none of them would ever come home or be seen again.

Our hearts were broken.

We cried as other nations wept with us. They honored our dead and flew our flag. They promised to stand by us.

Our hearts were broken.

Then, across our great nation, our flag began to appear. One by one they were hung everywhere! Through the tears we reached out to each other and now stand united, stronger than ever before.

Our hearts were broken, but they cannot break our spirit.

United we stand.

HEALING TOGETHER

21" x 28½" Sonia Callahan
Piedmont, CA USA

In the aftermath of the terrorist attacks, the sea of images that showed destruction and pain troubled me deeply. Finally, a local newspaper carried an image of people attending a burial service holding hands. I have tried to recreate a part of that image that recognizes our nation's sadness, but gives hope and confidence to the idea that Americans will unite to overcome.

STARS IN TEARS

30" x 30" Rosario Casanovas
Sant Feliu de Boada, Gerona Spain

"It makes me sad to see that human beings have the ability to cause so much pain." These were my husband's words after the events of 9/11, and this is my quilt.

America's sorrow is symbolized in Stars in Tears, *but tears were not only shed by Americans that day, but also by people in most countries throughout the world. Although the "tears" I've represented here unfortunately cannot help the victims and probably not their families, I hope they will make us more aware of the gift of life and the need of harmony and peace between all people.*

THE COLORS OF SEPTEMBER

22⅜" x 31¼" Linda Martire-Bollenbach
Winsted, CT USA

I am a native New Yorker. I worked in New York City during the construction of the World Trade Towers.

LIBERTY'S TORCH

14½" x 11¼" Karen Waechter
Lutz, FL USA

I designed the pattern of the Statue of Liberty's torch for a patriotic block challenge my Monday quilt group had in July. A drawing was held to see who would win all the blocks…I lost, but decided someday I would make the torch again for myself. After the tragedy of 9/11/2001 my thoughts turned to ways to show my patriotism. I helped make "no sew flags" for a local quilt shop. The proceeds from the sale of the flags were donated to the American Red Cross Disaster Relief Fund. When I received an e-mail about this exhibit, I combined the ideas above and created Liberty's Torch.

HEALING OUR HEARTS ONE STITCH AT A TIME

18½" x 23¼" Joann Wirth Johnson
Stilwell, KS USA

After September 11th, I couldn't work on my own fun projects any more. I started making baby quilts, which I sent to a relative who lives a few blocks from Ground Zero. She took them to her local firehouse, where many people were lost. After five baby quilts, I wanted to make something to commemorate the day, the outpouring of patriotism and love I saw all around me, and the sacrifices that are being made and will be made in the future by our military services (including my own brother). Each stitch I take helps me to come to grips with this series of unthinkable tragedies. While I won't keep this quilt, I plan to make another similar quilt for my family and myself.

AMERICA'S HEROES

26" x 25" Maxine Oliver
Yorktown Heights, NY USA

On September 11, 2001 as I was watching Simply Quilts my husband called from Manhattan, "Quick, put on the news." I did, and like everyone else, I sat in total shock and disbelief at the events that were happening right there before my eyes.

When I learned of the request for Memorial quilts for the Houston Show I knew I had to make one.

With tears in my eyes and a prayer in my heart I dedicate this quilt to the many victims of the terrorist attack on the World Trade Center, Pentagon, and Shanksville, PA. Especially to the brave men and women who gave their lives in the pursuit of saving others—FDNY, NYPD and the Port Authority Police—I dedicate this quilt. God Bless America.

MEMORIES AND HOPES

16" x 13" Karen Case
Granbury, TX USA

On the morning of September 11, 2001, my husband and I were watching the news while enjoying our morning coffee. Little did we know we would be eyewitnesses to the most horrifying and dastardly event in United States history. For two days, I was glued to the television as events continued to unfold. On the third day, I knew I had to do something or I would burst. I love to paper piece, but couldn't find a flag anywhere in my library. A wonderful lady, Christine Thresh, www.winnowing.com, placed a simple and elegant paper pieced flag on the internet as a free pattern as her way of sharing her feelings. This was perfect...MEMORIES ...in memory of innocent victims and fallen heroes.

After completing the flag, I turned to my stash for a border. My eyes immediately fell on the patriotic children print...HOPES...our hopes for the future. The piece was completed. However, I still felt very strongly in voicing what I was feeling ...and the cries being heard again and again over the networks, "God Bless America," "Let Freedom Ring," and "United We Stand."

ONE NATION

18½" x 12½" Lyric Kinard
Cary, NC USA

We are One Nation No matter where we came from
Under God No matter what name we give Him
With liberty and Justice for all none should fear for the sake of race or religion
We must stand United without Fear If we are to prevail
We will rise United!

NEW GROWTH

14" x 14" Del Thomas
Placentia, CA USA

From the terrifying events of September 11, 2001, comes a new belief in our country and the growth of mutual support and understanding. We must set aside hate and work together for our freedom.

THROUGH IT ALL

42" x 31" Karen Villa
Tonawanda, NY USA

When news of the first crash into the World Trade Center was announced we were on our way to Judy Dales, Quilt-Inn at Greensboro, VT. Judy was to teach us how to combine stars and curves in the same piece. I worried about my son and his family in Washington, D.C., my other children around the country, and the state of our country and the world.

I deeply felt America was hurt and bleeding. Images on the TV were horrific and difficult to comprehend. I knew God would see us through but still felt angry at what these people, filled with such hatred, had done.

This quilt is all the feelings of my heart on that day. I began the work September 12, 2001, and finished it October 22, 2001. The work was made difficult not because of the pieces but because of the emotions. With God's help, America will come through all of this stronger and closer. Through the flames on the right side of the quilt America emerges to defend freedom and our flag continues to wave. Four large stars are the four planes that went down. There are nine small and eleven medium stars for the date. GOD BLESS AMERICA!

A beautiful tribute to our country.

GIVE ME YOUR TIRED

35½" x 26" Susan McKenna
Honolulu, HI USA

The design of this quilt began shortly after learning of the disaster at 4:30 A.M. in Hawaii. It continued to be an image in my mind, evolving over the days after the event and finally taking shape to honor all those lost and those impacted. While talking with a co-worker who lost his sister in the Trade Center, I recall telling him that I can't imagine what he is going through, yet I can.

The hats salute the many relief workers whose feelings and emotions I can't imagine, yet I can.

The pentagons in the sky are for the families in Washington whose feelings I can't imagine, yet I can.

The quilting in the flag honors those lost in the gentle rolling hills of western Pennsylvania and for their families whose feelings I can't imagine, yet I can.

Yet we all can.

SPIRITS RISING

31" x 35" Betsy Shannon
Minneapolis, MN USA

I've always been able to fall asleep easily, until September 11, 2001. I started designing this quilt in my mind, to help me cope with the many emotions I felt, especially when trying to fall asleep, or when waking up at 4:00 A.M. from the feelings of grief and despair, and the nightmares.

As I started to sketch my ideas down on paper, the design began to take on a life of its own. My various images grew into representing patriotism, with the stars and stripes, and the ghost images of monuments that became the final resting place of so many individual people.

My deepest purpose of the design was to represent the souls of each of those people rising to another place, a better place, to a life beyond this one. I wanted the design to transcend organized religion, encompassing all beliefs, faiths, and walks of life, as a further representation of the many different people who lost their lives.

I found out about this exhibit on September 29, with the design still on paper. That night I put the design on cloth and made the commitment to get it done for the exhibit, the only way I could, by using fabric paints and machine quilting. I finished it in a week and a half.

AD COUNCIL QUILT OF CARE

72" x 46" The Advertising Council, Kelly McBride, coordinator
New York, NY USA

We arrived at work that morning to find that only a few miles away, the most horrible act of terrorism in history was taking place. We watched with disbelief at the images that were displayed on TV. Some of us watched from 5th Avenue, as the two buildings stood there burning before our eyes. Some rushed to leave the city when word got out that it was in a lockdown. Others had to walk hours from our office in Midtown to their homes in outside boroughs. In the days that followed, we gave blood, volunteered anywhere we could, gave financially, and cheered as the rescue workers drove down the West Side Highway. Weeks went by and we asked ourselves, "What can we do now?" After stumbling across this festival while looking for ways to help out on the Internet, it gave us an opportunity to do something creative and a way to give back. Before you is the end result of a week and a half of work. The quilt gave us a way to express the feelings that we have been dealing with since September 11th.

We will forever mourn those who were lost. We will forever take pride that we are Americans. We will forever live our life bravely and hope for a day where terrorism no longer exists. God Bless!

E Pluribus Unum

49" x 49" Beth Porter Johnson
Houston, TX USA

The quilt is a personal response to the terrorist attacks on the World Trade Center and the Pentagon. I experienced feelings of disbelief, horror, and anxiety. There was, however, a feeling of unity...and of pride in being an American. Hopefully this quilt will serve as a reminder that our strength together is greater than our individual differences.

The clasped hands represent all those who stand together against tyranny. The translucent hand, symbolizing those who died in the attacks and in the rescue efforts that followed, reaches out to unite in spirit with the others. The title—the motto of the United States—translates, "Out of Many, One."

Hands of Friendship 9-11

91" x 75" Nancy Loftis and the Desert Quilters
Temecula, CA USA

In the aftermath of the events of September 11th, it was difficult to resume our lives without acknowledging the horrific injury inflicted upon America. Feelings of disbelief, for the children who have been robbed of their innocence. Feelings of grief for the families who have lost loved ones, whose lives and world have been turned upside down. Anger for those who may yet lose loved ones, and the oppressed and innocent. And lastly, relief, because we have a renewed fervor to preserve those freedoms for which this country was founded.

O'er the Land of the Free

22" x 17" Susanne McCoy
Washington, D.C. USA

I was unsure how I would capture the many mixed feelings and reactions to September 11th, so I started as I do when I turn to sewing as a healing, or meditative activity. I began to cut and piece red strips with no particular plan in mind. As this process continued, it's not surprising that the result is my version of Old Glory. We live just five miles from the Pentagon, and while we've known the reality of being under curfew, and military planes overhead, it has been a breathtakingly beautiful fall.

This fall, the sight that brings me comfort as I drive or walk around the city is the huge number of flags flying from houses, cars and store windows. I grieve for all the victims and their families, and I am proud of our country's unified response.

GOD BLESS AMERICA

29" x 28½" Deanna Augustin
Shelby, NE USA

I feel privileged and yet deeply saddened to be a part of this special AMERICA: From the Heart exhibit.

I don't know of any words or design that can possibly express all my feelings.

In this Mary Graham design we see the rolling green countryside of Pennsylvania. In the foreground the Pentagon, the World Trade Center and a fireman representing all the emergency personnel involved in this shocking tragedy. Through it all, our flag waves. I added the four crosses to the right of the World Trade Center to commemorate the innocent lives lost on those four airplanes.

Eventually I plan to give this to our local Volunteer Fire Department for their meeting room, lest we forget.

LOVE AND PRAYERS

73" x 86" Janet Byram Newsom
Marshall, TX USA

My husband and I were on our 50th birthday Alaskan cruise when we learned of the September 11th tragedy. I found myself sitting in front of the television, praying, crying, and designing quilt tops. I made this quilt the week after I arrived home. The hearts are representative of the love and people we lost that day, but also of the love manifested by the United States for each other. In loss, we found faith, love, and courage to meet this crisis. The quilted hearts and stars are symbolic of the lives lost. The quilted hands in the border remind us we must reach out to each other each day, not to wait for tragedy.

I would like to give special thanks to Gail Thomas of Quilter's Corner in Jefferson, TX for the expedited quilting. The freehand machine quilting came from her soul.

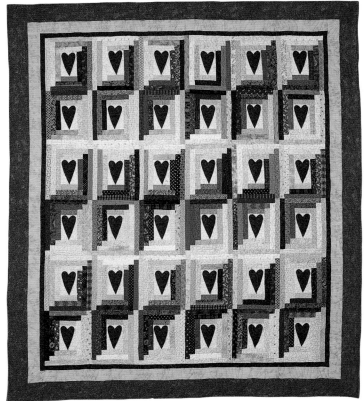

9/11 LEST WE FORGET

22" x 24" Cathy Isdale
Houston, TX USA

I was raised a Texan and grew up with the motto, "Remember the Alamo." Now as a patriotic American my new motto is "9/11 and the World Trade Center. We must forgive but not forget."

We need to be ever vigilant. We must know that our God has given us the free will to choose good in our lives and not evil.

The ones who chose evil will regret it. As America's might and strength will mobilize against the evil, we will hold our heads high and love our land and freedoms. God Bless America.

Hearts on the mend!

JUSTICE LIFTS A NATION

32" x 27" Deborah S. Reed
Graham, WA USA

As the events of September 11th unfolded, sorrow washed over my soul like the waves of the ocean.
I could not get the woeful images of the death and destruction out of my mind, and I set out to portray them in fabric. As I worked... I went without sleep at times and skipped meals; I wept and felt chills run up and down my spine as I listened to the news and continued to sew.

Lady Justice, inspired by a fresco, Justice Lifts A Nation, in the Old Supreme Court Building in Lausanne, Switzerland, holds scales in one hand. A sword in her other hand points to God's word, the basis for law and government. The ancient architecture is juxtaposed against the modern metropolis with its two tall towers and tragic rubble below. The serene blue sky and "Old Glory" represent the feeling of unwavering hope I have for the future of a country that promises liberty and justice for all.

EYES OF TARA

27" x 34" Dara Tokarz
Sedona, AZ USA

As the events of 9/11 unfolded, prayer was one of the only ways of coping with the shock and horror. The need to do something was overwhelming, and I began designing this quilt. In the quilt's original design, the towers were a part of the backdrop...I decided it needed to be more of a testament. Will we ever be able to look at the New York skyline without seeing the memory of those buildings? The one-inch squares ...soon came to represent the various nations affected. The doves represent each of the four doomed flights. The earth represents the fact that this was not only an American tragedy, but a global one. And the eyes of Tara—Angel of Peace, Mother of Compassion——because it is my fervent prayer that our connection with whatever matriarchal energy we revere...will bring us to our ultimate goal, PEACE.

OM TARE TU TARE TURE SOHA

COMMON THREADS

37" x 28" Chris Griffin Pascuzzi
Virginia Beach, VA USA

On September 11, 2001 our nation was changed forever. Landmarks were lost and damaged. Thousands of innocent people lost their lives because of a sick and misguided hatred. The heart of America was broken.

Yet on the same day heroes were born. Some wore uniforms. Others were just everyday folks. Different people connected by common threads. The crisp white banners are covered with words that to me represent America at its best. They are a strong contrast to the ragged edges of the heart and the edges of the quilt itself. The silver stars stand for the heroes.

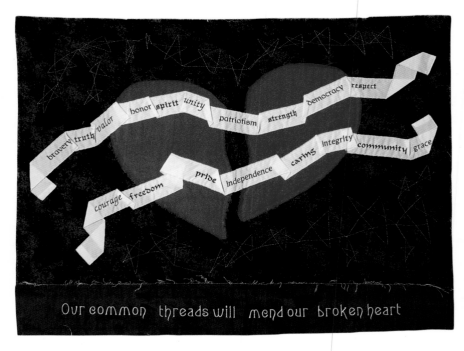

FOR YOU

17" x 17" Suzanne Armstrong
San Antonio, TX USA

I found it hard to simplify the chaotic images that have been before us since September 11th in order to put something down. I cannot stop thinking about the tremendous loss to our country and to so many individual people. I chose the shape of the World Trade Center because it looks like a crown, the crown of liberty attacked, a heart for the way people have been treating each other and the stars for the missing souls that light the sky. Deep purple is for healing, golden yellow for light, red for love.

UNITED WE STAND

35" x 50" Judith Brainerd
Olympia, WA USA

I grew up during the Civil Rights Movement of the 50s and 60s and the Vietnam War. The way I saw it, America had always been divided: those for, those against. Yet in one short moment, this country was united in a way I've never seen before. The tragedies of September 11th felt as though they had happened to all of us.

Within a week of the attacks, I began to design my quilt. I wanted to show the way I felt—that we are just one big neighborhood; that when one of us is cut, all of us bleed. So I took landmark buildings and monuments and put them into the New York skyline.

Buildings from left to right: Space Needle, Seattle, Washington; Golden Gate Bridge, San Francisco, California; Gateway Arch, St. Louis, Missouri Hancock Place, Boston, Massachusetts; Sears Tower, Chicago, Illinois; Chrysler Building, New York City, New York; Washington Monument, Washington, D.C.; West Quoddy Head Light, Lubec, Maine

FIVE THOUSAND SEVEN HUNDRED FORTY-SEVEN STARS

18" x 15" Dorothy Anguish
Vergennes, VT USA

When my children were babies, I would often sing You are my Sunshine to them, as they were falling asleep. Losing my sunshine seemed then, and still does now, to be an unimaginable, unbearable emptiness. But when the sun sets, we see the light is not gone, it is different. We can see the stars.

On September 11, 2001, many families had their sunshine taken from them. 5,747 people transformed from sunshine to starlight. Nine of them are children…

The spirits of these nine children are not lost. They have become stars in my sky. Like my grieving for these children, my quilt is not finished. I'm not sure it will ever be done.

BUILDING BONES: REMEMBERING THE TOWERS

28" x 33" Michele Merges Martens
Watervliet, NY USA

Journal entry September 10, 2001: on the way to Kyle's dance practice, the light, oh, the light—that golden overlay making the bricks a mellow deep coral and the tree leaves motionless and the air so still, waiting for something to happen

Journal entry September 11, 2001: Heaven must have been busy today. I can't understand why these tragedies happened, no one else can either. I feel guilty to be alive, to still be able to tell my stories, accomplish my dreams, solve my problems. They can't. The workers, the firemen, the policemen, the volunteers they will always be missed, they will always be mourned, they will always be remembered.

October 22, 2001: It's done. I see gravestones, building bones, structures to be rebuilt. I feel grief, still, but I am also able to create, to become renewed, to enjoy the sunshine again.

LIBERTY WEEPS FOR HER COUNTRY

34" x 44" Susan Shie
Wooster, OH USA

My quilt is about wanting peace in the face of chaos. Offering beauty where you see only death and destruction. Lady Liberty here is an angel, offering up two red roses of peace. Her crown is upside down, as a sign of distress, at the top of the image, with a large eye of God, or maybe the soul of our country, watching over us and our crisis. At the bottom of the quilt are two snakes, the stealth and deceit of the attackers…

Along the edges of the quilt are antique tension clothespins…These remind us of a happier time. The dull colored buttons remind us of the hard work that has been done and will continue, to rescue and clean up from the attack. Faces of…angels, as our friends and family. In the sky are blue pearl buttons…to represent our military, who are all so fully affected by the attacks. And on Liberty's shoulders are signs of balance and peace, for these things have always been part of the United States' promise to the world.

May things get back to balance and peace, more than ever, soon. Soon!

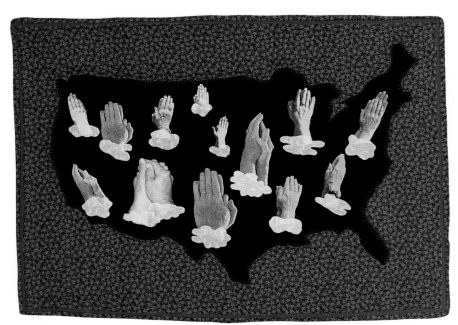

PRAYERS ACROSS AMERICA

38½" x 28" Eden Quilt Guild
Grammy Bees
Eden, NY USA

America is united in prayer, no matter what age, color or station in life.

Joanne Eckhardt, Mary Jo Hodge, Lucille Kornacki, Sheila Landon, Edwina Leas, Joan Staby, and Katy Sturm

AND A BILLION TEARS BEGAN TO FALL

30" x 30" Rosanna Lynne Welter
West Valley City, UT USA

I could not believe my eyes, staring at the big screen TV in our downtown mall on September 11th. The normally bustling food court—usually so full of activity, clattering dishes, and office workers chatting as they picked up a morning snack—was hushed. People drifted in, like sleepwalkers, found a chair, and watched in stunned disbelief as the never-to-be-forgotten events of that morning unfolded.

Incomprehensible cruelty occurred before our eyes. I did not try to hide my emotions from the many people gathered there, in such a public place, and neither did anyone else. …That morning, our tears flooded the world. Tears crossed borders, leveled classes, bridged differences, eliminated barriers, ended discords, mended relationships, sought new beginnings, and tried—oh, tried so desperately—to empty our hearts of the terrible sadness.

And finally, I think it was our tears that united us.

DAY OF DARKNESS

35½" x 36½" Jeri Riggs
Dobbs Ferry, NY USA

On a beautiful blue day in September, the world was plunged into darkness by acts of terrorism. Worries about my dear husband— who came out of the subway a block away from the World Trade Center, and looked up to see clouds of smoke and fire in the sky. There was a whirling, twinkling mass of paper falling around him. Making this quilt provided me with a way of actualizing my wish for love to conquer hatred. The skyline is broken but the eagle rises from the smoke and ruins into a cloud of hearts as goodness overshadows evil. Candles illuminate the darkness and remind us that our flickering spirits burn despite some being extinguished. May peace prevail.

THE VIGIL

43" x 38" Sally Beaton
Sarnia, ON Canada

Quilt Inn provided the perfect opportunity to channel the anger and grief that were the natural outgrowth of events of September 11th into something positive. It is almost prophetic that the planned subject of the seminar—stars and curves—lent itself so well to the creation of my quilt. The final design shows the sky-line of Manhattan, Lady Liberty's torch next to it, the stars, which represent the explosions, surrounded by smoke and flames, and finally the star of hope and the dove of peace keeping vigil through it all.

My quilt arose from the depths of my gut and captured the images that were in my mind. I am proud that I could take my emotions and my love for our country and our way of life, and turn them into something beautiful to give back to the world in remembrance. It was a catharsis for me, and a rebirth of my faith and hope.

You touched the heart of what makes us so fragile, human, and connected

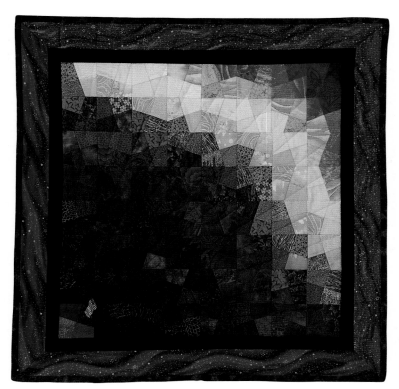

BROKEN RAINBOWS

26" x 26" Dianne Anderson
Tomball, TX USA

The idea for this quilt came from the block name, Broken Rainbows (Nancy Cabot, 1937). It reflects that our perception of the world was shattered for a moment, on September 11, 2001, and it, along with the New York skyline, looked pretty dark. Though we might still be a little shaken, we're not by any means broken.

The fabric in the lower left quadrant of the quilt was chosen to represent the lives lost and the rubble at Ground Zero, along with our national symbol of hope and pride, raised by the firemen.

This quilt is dedicated to those victims of hatred and violence, and to the memories of the heroes, both the known and the unknown, on the ground and in the air, who gave their lives for their fellow man, regardless of race, creed, or nationality.

DONA NOBIS PACEM

18" x 27" Susanne Slesinger
Seal Beach, CA USA

In the days that followed the attacks I tried to regain my equilibrium by listening to sacred music and requiems composed during the last millennium. The music helped my soul while inspiring me.

The words from the Latin liturgy Dona Nobis Pacem *and* Dona Eis Requiem *kept going round in my head and I decided to express them in fabric. The center* Dona Nobis Pacem (give us peace) *is surrounded by the text* Memoria in aeterna (in eternal memory). *The lower panel depicts our country turned upside down and inside out by the events of September 11th. The partial black dove at the bottom represents our initial faltering steps to recover. The lightening and growth of the dove until it again becomes the white dove symbolic of peace represents our recovery from the tragedies. The upper panel represents the completed rebuilding process where lights will shine and stars will spread their rays over us.*

The borders contain both embroidered and quilted words for peace in many languages and dialects of indigenous people from Albanian to Zulu. Many of the quotes were sent by friends from international internet quilting groups. The design for the label was digitized by an Australian.

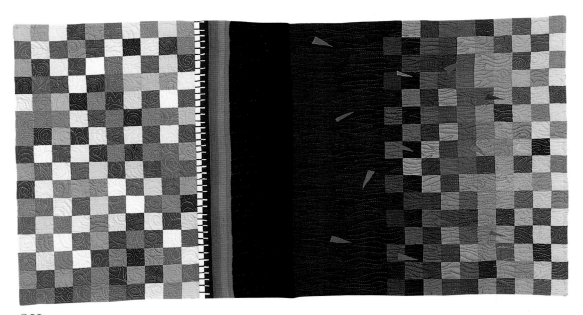

911

43¼" x 22½" Mary Beth Goodman
Brainard, NY USA

The phone rang on 9/11/01. I listened to my mother talking and prepared to hear that someone had died. Who could have imagined? We didn't have a TV where we were so we didn't get the barrage of instant images. All we could do is listen to the phoned reports and wonder.

What stuck me about that day was the change. The sky was crystal blue, the Adirondack water still sparkled with the sun, the mountains still held in the lake on all sides. What had changed was me. I felt that someone had knocked a hole in my body or head...I looked at the others and they seemed to have the same problem putting themselves into this new existence.

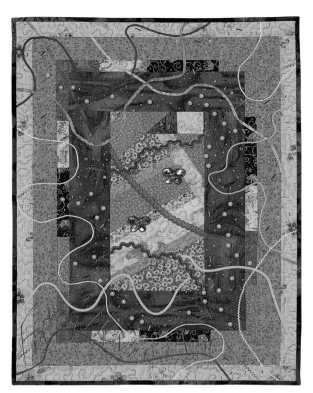

FINDING MY WAY, AGAIN

23½" x 31½" Kim King
Perry Township, OH USA

*I'm still not able to process my feelings about the attack.
At first, I felt a quiet detachment, as if what was happening
would never affect me. Then, as I watched the horrid scenes
of the suicide missions, I realized that my life might change in
profound ways. I am saddened by the vastness of the destruction
and I am scared about my future…I am distracted; I find it very
difficult to concentrate on my work.*

My latest quilt, Finding My Way, Again *has taken on new meaning
for me. Now, when I look at my finished quilt, I see that my country,
my government, also has choices to make. America needs to find
its way out of this crisis.*

COLLISION COURSE

57" x 43½" Nancy Hinds
Covington, LA USA

*All the film and photographs of New York City after the
World Trade Center towers fell were gray—this is my color
interpretation of those desolate scenes. The "creatures"
represent the unknown terror among us, while the triangle
and candle in the center show that hope and strength should
be our focus. We will not let this horrible event disrupt our
lives completely.*

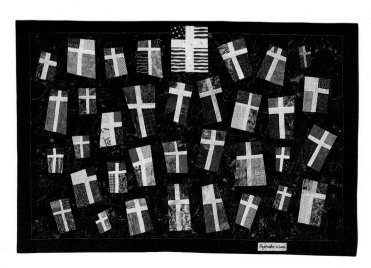

SEPTEMBER 11, 2001

59" x 41" Marguerite L. B. Crum
West Lafayette, IN USA

*Everyone will always remember where they were
when they heard the terrible news of September 11th.
The enormity and its implications were immediate
and overwhelming.*

*I knew I had to direct my energy into a quilt. I pulled
out fabrics randomly and haphazardly made crosses.
This is far from my usual precise and planned style
of creating but it fit the frenzied mood of the day.
While I sewed I watched the events unfold.*

*All along, I had known it would be quilted with the
Lord's Prayer, the first words out of my mouth upon
hearing the news.*

When We Touch Common Ground

11" x 31" Rita Zerull
Escondido, CA USA

In my lifetime, I have seen four wars that involved my country. I have seen in the newspapers and on TV accounts of the many cruelties and violent acts committed in my country and around the world. The list is endless! This latest horrible event is burned into my brain. These many days of sorrow and far too many other times have caused me to cry oceans of tears. But through these tears, I have seen so much courage, kindness and faith. I find hope in the outpouring of generosity and support, not only from Americans, but also from people around the world. Out of this sorrow perhaps everyone will embrace one another, not because of race, religion, color, or country but because we all live on this beautiful planet called Earth. That is why my quilt is titled When We Touch Common Ground. *We all spring from the same ground so we should embrace one another, because all we have is each other. God bless our family, the human race!*

I feel truly humbled and yet spiritually thrilled at all I have seen.

All That We Are

30" x 30" Sherry Boram
Pendleton, IN USA

While I was making this quilt, the tangle of emotions I felt about the events of September 11th gave way to these ideas: Honor the victims, rescuers and survivors. (The pentagon, twin rectangles, and keystone shapes, the tear-shaped quilting); All peoples of the planet are affected. (All colors are used.); A higher purpose is at work here. (America IS blessed. May God bless ALL.); We are in this together. (Let's live, love and learn. Let's join hands as a nation, as a world.)

All…that we are, All that…we are.

September 2001

21" x 30" Cindy McLeod
Ringgold, GA USA

The horror of the terrorist attacks was their brutal reminder of how quickly life can take a 180° turn from peace and prosperity into war and anxiety.

During those early awful days before tears even came, I kept thinking of a quotation from Anne Frank that was on the bulletin board in the classroom in which I volunteer. I was struck by how wise this young girl had been. She looked straight into the darkness, with no illusions about its nature, and yet saw beyond it. Light and darkness are both part of our world. Like Anne, I have to believe the light will return. Even now in the middle of this uncertainty and worry, I find hope in acts of heroism and kindness. If we can appreciate our family and friends more, find satisfaction not in what we have but in what we give, and reach out to those who are different from ourselves, we will overcome those who want to destroy us.

Americans United

8" x 15" Larkin Van Horn
Freeland, WA USA

After many hours of watching the news unfold, I sought the solace of my studio. I simply could not take in any more images and needed to deal with those that I had.

One thought kept returning: the terrorists chose two airlines whose very names spoke to our national identity—American and United. And Americans were, indeed, United: in grief, in outrage, in shock, and in resolve. It was in hearing the stories of the courage shown by the passengers and crews aboard the four planes that prepared me for the serendipity that occurred on the cutting table.

The quilting is meant to represent the rubble and the layers of dust and debris. The beads were added to represent the names of the passengers and crews—much like the names carved in stone for other memorials—unreadable until you get up close. The column itself stands tall and proud in the midst of destruction. Here were people who knew what was happening to them, and showed amazing courage in the face of certain death.

May we all be blessed with similar courage, resolve, and pride as we face the future together—Americans United.

COMMON THREADS OF LOVE

73" x 82" Lisa Wolf Guajardo
Katy, TX USA

Common Threads of Love *not only combines my new found love of quilting with my long lasting love for my husband, but also my profound love of my country. America, with its beautiful flag of red, white, and blue and* The Pledge of Allegiance *inspired this quilt, my first design.*

We are Americans, thankful for the privilege we have to live our lives as our founding fathers felt that all free people should live. Our flag, as the single most recognizable symbol of what the United States stands for, was the focal point of the quilt. The twelve flags rest on a continuous refrain of The Pledge of Allegiance, *constantly reminding us again and again of who and what we are as Americans...*

NEW YORK, NEW YORK 10048

84" x 75" Christine Bagley
Middletown, RI USA

I was born in Queens, New York and raised in New York but I spent the last twenty years of my life as a navy wife, moving from coast to coast in the United States. I feel a loss on many levels. I started this Memorial quilt on September 11, 2001 because the World Trade Center had its own zip code. It was not a building or a symbol, but a community of Americans going about their lives. Forty-nine blocks represent the states other than New York. My vision ran from a clear, beautiful Tuesday morning in America, through the attack on our lives.

The skies around us have changed, but there is the inevitable arrival, with faith, of each new dawn.

HELP/FEAR

26" x 39½" Barbara Pucci
Brooklyn, NY USA

By 9:30 A.M. on 9/11/01, paper and ash from the World Trade Center were raining on Brooklyn. Dropping out of the sky were pieces of résumés, hedge fund prospectuses, and investment information. As I watched the paper flutter to the ground I wondered what the authors of these pages would write about now if they could. Would they be asking for help? Or would they describe their fear?

As I watched the smoke slowly clear and unveil the gaping hole in the NYC skyline, I was unable to stop feeling helpless and afraid for the future. In the days that followed, feeling paralyzed, I forced myself to start working on a new piece—this piece—in an attempt to unlock myself and find movement again...I began trying to print a scroll, a kind of prayer shawl, to speak for those of us that are getting caught in the crossfire. The only words that felt right were the different ways of saying, help *and* fear.

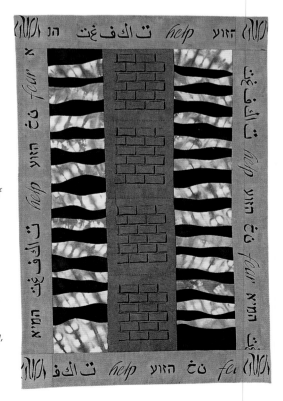

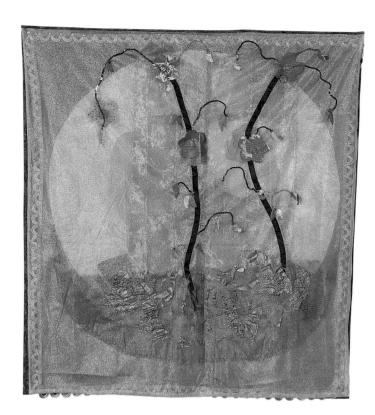

OUT OF THE ASHES

45" x 54" Sharona Fischrup
Piedmont, CA USA

Both my brothers gone from my life—both towers gone. How do you say goodbye to a brother? Two brothers? A whole working community of brothers and sisters? What is one death or one separation, with so many?

This quilt was born in spurts of inspiration—first was the fabric I found, it reminded me of the towers...then the photo of my brothers, at peace, alive whole, well, together, a few years back, came to mind. Then the towers, filmy over the photo, the images of my brothers. Then, what?

Out of the ashes, something grew...a faint something, nature in a healing mode. After the cleansing, the clearing of the destruction, the counting of the dead, the honoring of the lives of those connected with this horror...came growth.

*A beautiful display
with meaning for all.*

RENEWAL

19½" x 18¼" Rosemary Claus-Gray
Doniphan, MO USA

This single dogwood flower, blooming out of the ashes, offers hope and beauty to restore one's soul. It is a reminder that life will go on, in spite of unimaginably terrible experiences like the terrorist attacks on September 11, 2001 in America. This quilt expresses the hope of life emerging from a stark and barren place, when it does not seem possible that life can be good or beautiful again.

In spite of tragedy, turmoil and pain in the world, when I see something in nature that is exquisitely beautiful, I am reminded that all is right with God. The dogwood represents the eternal hope of spring. It brings us a healing message of faith, and evidence of the existence of God. May peace be with you.

WITH LIBERTY AND JUSTICE FOR ALL
28½" x 36½" Carol Yingst
Kadena Air Base, Okinawa, Japan

Within the first twenty-four hours after the attack on America, I received a very strong and beautiful vision merging the Statue of Liberty with Our Lady of Guadalupe. As I worked on the quilt, her meaning kept unfolding for me. She seems to be Mother Earth, not stoppable by anger, surprise or sadness with the current state of things, but full of knowledge, wisdom, and determination to protect us from small-minded thinking…The oppression of women in Afghanistan shows us exactly what happens when this balance is out of whack.

Liberty usually holds a book in her hand, now she holds the human child we must educate. All action must take into consideration the planet's children's children, for it is their world we are creating. And her torch is no longer just for people who yearn to be free, but for those who have not yet learned such an option exists. The torch has been thrown to those of us who have been blessed by the sacrifices of those who have come before us.

COMPASSION GIVING COMFORT
48" x 60" Pamela Allen
Kingston, ON Canada

Although I have been experimenting with fabric as an art medium for about a year, I had never actually made a quilt. I felt the events of 9/11 compelling me to embark on my first effort to use the quilt as an artistic expression. I have used fabric from a wide range of sources, Salvation Army resurrections, pieces given to me by helpful friends on various quilting lists, and pieces salvaged from my own clothing. They began to represent the universal involvement of all of us in this tragedy. My message is that we seek peace, help each other and conduct our lives with compassion.

IF WE ALL FOUGHT WARS WITH STRAWBERRIES, WE WOULDN'T BE IN THIS JAM

68" x 94½" Betty Betke
Bardstown, KY USA

On September 11, 2001, the country of my birth and the city of my birth were brutally attacked, and may never be the same. The television allowed me to experience it so vividly that I could not stop screaming. When I finally stopped screaming, I couldn't stop crying. I began to work on a quilt, as a way to express my feelings and to keep myself from living in total despair. This is the result. I call it a Peace Quilt. I will continue making Peace Quilts until it's no longer necessary. Why did I use a humorous approach? Humor is the flip side of pain. Sometimes it helps people to cope with a situation...This is not to say that I minimize the importance of what is happening to our country now. But it might help us expand our thinking and realize that there may be alternatives to warfare. I wish you peace in your lifetime.

Thank you for the stitches from the heart.

LIBERTY LOOKS OUT

30" x 40" Kenna Gene Dees
San Marcos, TX USA

The telephone is a metaphor for all those that were lost in the terrorist attack—so many voices silenced forever. The peace sign background is my wish that we all find eventual harmony. Liberty is the power within all of us to look out and radiate that America is united.

THE TRINITY

45" x 40" Norma DeHaven
Fitchburg, WI USA

I had been having a much more difficult time with the events of September 11, 2001 than I would have ever expected. I would break into tears every other hour—I was mourning someone I loved, and I didn't know who it was yet. I had difficulty sleeping for nights on end— waking to terrible nightmares about planes and flying. I turned to my church that week, several times, and found some relief. But I still couldn't shake the feelings of disbelief, anger, and sadness.

Then, on Sunday, September 16th, I went into my studio and didn't re-emerge until this piece was designed and the top was sewn. I slept all night that night. "Things come in threes," my mother often said. I wanted to use three images to help the healing. The cross, representing the people who lost their lives…Second is the country represented, of course, by the red, white, and blue stripes. The last, is my faith's trinity of the Father, Son, and Holy Spirit, represented by the circular shapes and the Sun. This is the most important "three" of all.

INDIVISIBLE

25" x 25" Deb Ecklund
Ben Lomond, CA USA

The ribbons were chosen from the Olympic rings to symbolize international flag colors. The gray is for the cloud of mourning. The black and white symbolize right and wrong. The children represent all nations and races.

RAINBOW OF HOPE

12" x 24" Rachelle Gorland
Lancaster, OH USA

The globe to me is a smorgasbord of music, art, dance, animals, climates, architecture, food, technology…which I have sampled in my quilting motifs. I would like to see us unite as "citizens of the world" while we celebrate our respective patriotism and culture. I view rainbows as a promise of good things to come. My rainbow is bands of love, peace, and hope. I pray we may all be blessed with peace, love, and joy.

SEPTEMBER 11, 2001

70" x 70" Frieda Grischkowsky
Stillwater, OK USA

Working on this quilt served as a therapy to help me deal with my profound feelings of sadness, helplessness and anger over what happened on September 11th. I wanted to make a strong symbolic statement with my design choices and color scheme. God Bless America.

A SINGLE TOWER

16¾" x 55½" Denise A. Currier
Mesa, AZ USA

"In The Form of Art"
In the wake of what
has occurred
Apart from the
process of healing
Remember we specialize
in expressing our feelings
Such as a physical hug,
cooking, cleaning or even running
We, are capable of expressing
in the form of Art
May it be sewing, painting, drawing,
writing or by performing in music
These are the gifts that keep on giving
These are, the packages from our hearts

9-11 A CALL FOR HOPE

48" x 48" Cynthia Geist and Carol Bird Riffe
Brighton, MI USA

Reflecting upon the aftermath in the weeks after 9/11, we are inspired by the quotation from Anne Frank: "I don't think of all the misery, but of the beauty that still remains. My advice to you is: go outside, to the fields, enjoy nature and the sunshine, go out and try to recapture the happiness in yourself and in God. Think of all the beauty that's still left in and around you and be happy."

As we began to realize the good things that had already begun to happen, we opened a dialogue with our friends and relatives, asking them for words and phrases of the positive changes they were noticing in our country. Many of these words are quilted into the stems of the flowers in our design, as a tangible reminder of the power of hope. The dove is a universal symbol of peace, our hope for the future.

SHINE

14¼" x 34" Elin Waterston
South Salem, NY USA

As the horrific events of September 11th unfolded, I found myself unable to grasp, or bear, the magnitude of the loss of human life. I began to mourn not only for the thousands of shattered lives, but also for the city itself... I have chosen to represent the World Trade Center in that light and to celebrate its brilliance. I hope that the survivors of that day, and the families and friends of those who were so brutally murdered in New York, Washington D.C., and Pennsylvania will be able to remember the beauty of life as it once was. May the memory of those lost continue to shine, always.

EARTH QUILT #102: CELEBRATION OF LIFE XXIV

50½" x 50½" Meiny Vermaas-Van Der Heide
Tempe, AZ USA

The many quilts in my Celebration of Life series have always tried to express the fragility and preciousness of life...The black and white fabrics are like scribbles in the pages of a diary. The colorful squares stand for the happy times with our children; the red squares stand for emotions. Paralyzed by the attacks I decided to celebrate the lives of all men and women who lost theirs with this quilt...The topstitching of tessellating crosses is done in rainbow colors representing hope and promise for the future by holding together in dealing with this tragedy.

I CRIED, I PRAYED

20½" x 24½" Jodie-Marie Horne
Leduc, Alberta Canada

On September 11th, I cried and I prayed for all the people who lost their lives. I prayed to God to protect those still alive amid the destruction, for those searching for family, friends and fellow workers. I prayed for God to safely lead his children home. And I cry. And I pray.

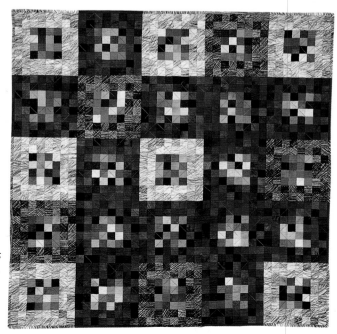

WAR AND PEACE

30" x 23" Ann Louise Mullard-Pugh
Las Vegas, NV USA

On another September the 11th, in 1793, Benjamin Franklin wrote in a letter to Josiah Quency, "There was never a good war or a bad peace." Two parties enter into a conflict, each sure they have right on their side and that the other is completely wrong, misguided, and evil. There are never simple answers to complex questions...perhaps that is why there is still war...no matter how carefully we pursue the guilty, innocent people—mostly women and children—will suffer. May military helmets soon be the nesting sites for the doves of peace.

911 MEMORIAL: A GIFT FROM JAPAN

96" x 84" Yuko Sakurai and Yoko Akimoto
Representing quilters from Japan. Kanagawa-ken, Japan

Immediately after the attacks on September 11th, we felt an overwhelming need to express our sympathy to the citizens of the United States and to console the families of the victims.

As quilters, we have a strong connection to America. When American patchwork was introduced to our country, we learned the skills of quilting and the lessons of hospitality associated with this craft. Now, in return for this great gift, we would like to send our message of peace and hope to all Americans.

Through the Internet, 340 quilters were contacted to join this project. Within two weeks, quilt blocks arrived from all over Japan. The blocks all contain a message of love for each child affected by the events of 911.

September 11, 2001

20" x 28" Judy Coates Perez
Austin, TX USA

I found it very difficult to find words to explain the imagery on my quilt; however, I made the quilt as a spiritual snapshot capturing this moment in history.

Serenity

36" x 27" Sarah Williams
Menomonee Falls, WI USA

In the last year I lost two very important people in my life. I was in mourning when the quilt came together at Haystack with Elizabeth Busch. I found serenity and hope within the piece when I finished it.

The Angels Cried

22" x 44" Amy Linn
Dupree, SD USA

I believe that we are constantly surrounded by angels, who guide and watch over our daily lives. Some of these angels are heavenly beings that constantly working to keep us safe. Some of them reside in human form, and they are sometimes in the most unexpected places...we meet for a moment and never see again.

On September 11, 2001 the angels were busy, they worked hard and diligently to protect and save so many people. In the stories we read about strangers helping others down many flights of stairs, the emergency medical technicians, firemen and policemen, the people on the planes who were able to keep calm and calm others around them, we saw those angels, and we felt the presence of angels unseen...But in the midst of all that darkness, in the hearts and in the lives of all of us, a light still burns brightly...it is a light of hope and a light of peace.

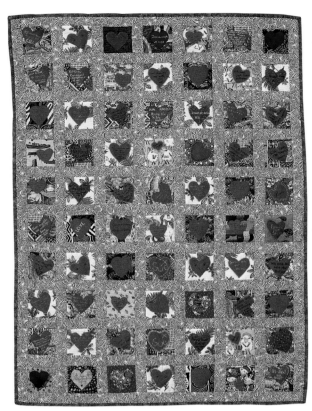

WITH LOVE FROM NEW ZEALAND

**39" x 54" New Zealand quilters,
Helen Marshall, coordinator**
Raumati Beach, Kapiti Coast New Zealand

This quilt was made, by many New Zealand quilters and their friends as a gesture of sympathy to our American friends for the 11th of September tragedy. For this quilt the blocks were bordered with a New Zealand fern pattern fabric (our national symbol). The back of the quilt has squares of black and white fabrics which are our national colours and is signed by the quilters who turned the blocks into quilts.

In one week I received 224 blocks after my request to my New Zealand Quilting internet contacts, and with some friends, we made two quilts.

Heartfelt & healing: an amazing array of anguish, love, and hope.

FROM THE HEARTS OF NEW ZEALAND

**44" x 63" New Zealand quilters,
Helen Marshall, coordinator**
Raumati Beach, Kapiti Coast New Zealand

This quilt was made and assembled and quilted by many New Zealand quilters, their families and friends, as a gesture of sympathy to our American friends for the 11th of September tragedy.

The black and white (our national colours) New Zealand fabric represents the New Zealand side of the Pacific Ocean and the multi coloured New Zealand fabrics the American side of the Pacific Ocean. The map of New Zealand is made with fern fabric to represent our national symbol. The back of the quilt has squares of black and white fabrics and is signed by the quilters who turned the blocks into quilts.

In one week I received 224 blocks after my request to my New Zealand quilting Internet contacts and with some friends we made up two quilts.

THE FIRST HERO

28" x 24" Cathy Cloud

Port Aransas, TX USA

Todd Beamer refused to stay in his seat aboard United Flight 93 on September 11th. Having learned from an in-flight telephone operator what was happening in New York and Washington D.C., Todd and other passengers decided to challenge the terrorists. Todd's last words were "...let's roll."

This moving display brings tears to our eyes but joy to our spirits.

SILVER AND GREEN AND GOLD

30" x 20" Paula Newquist

Madison, AL USA

On Wednesday, September 12, 2001, I woke up to a beautiful, bright sunny day. There was a hint of fall in the air. One of my first thoughts was of a family grace that my mother taught us as children. As I went for an early morning walk, it reverberated through my head. The dogwood trees were just starting to turn color, and they had bright red berries from last year's flowers and the buds that promise to be flowers next year. What a metaphor of hope. I had started making a small quilt with the grace on it when I took a workshop from Laura Cater-Woods. I showed her the work in progress and was thinking that it needed something more. I was thinking a tree line at the bottom of the quilt but as soon as Laura suggested leaves, I knew that it had to be the dogwood branches.

CELESTIAL EULOGY

40" x 30" Christine Wenz
Cedar Park, TX USA

As a transplanted New Yorker living in Texas, I was horrified to see the terror and devastation that took place in New York and across our country. I watched the Towers being built. I visited the top on so many special occasions and now they are gone. I, like so many others, did not know what to do with myself…I needed to do something and making a quilt seemed to be the right thing…I tried to show how connected each one was and how they were tied together as mothers, fathers, brothers, sisters, lovers, and neighbors. Ordinary people, having lived ordinary lives, yet heroes to us all.

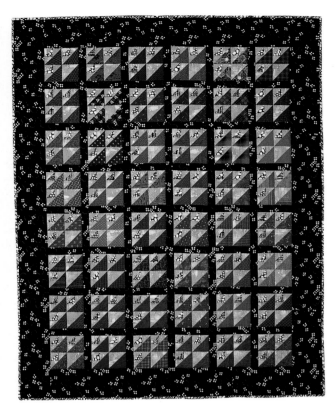

SEPTEMBER II, 2001

70¾" x 90¾" George Taylor and Judy Dafoe Hopkins
Anchorage, AK USA

We made this quilt while watching news coverage of the terrorist attack on the World Trade Center in New York and the Pentagon in Washington, D.C. The name of the traditional block used in the quilt is Airplane.

STAND UP FOR AMERICA

26¾" x 19½" Wanita Morrow
Osceola, MO USA

This quilt was Inspired by our many patriotic songs such as our national anthem, The Star-Spangled Banner, God Bless America and my favorite, I'm proud to be an American. *Indeed, I am proud to be an American. Proud to be the wife of a retired United States Air Force officer and especially proud to be the mother of a son who is a career officer currently serving in the United States Air Force. God Bless the USA!*

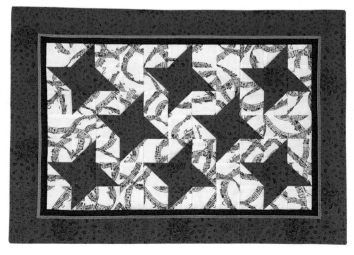

CITY LIGHTS

89" x 98" Lorraine Karl
Plano, TX USA

This quilt is for "Bob," brother, son, uncle to a family that is very proud and very grateful. It is being brought to him, in New York City, on Thanksgiving Day 2001. My quilts are made with love and hugs for family. Bob's quilt was begun in late August. September 11th and Bob's involvement changed the concept and content forever. The flag fabric has been mended, yet the quilt and our flag are whole.
Our hearts and country need to find ways to also mend. New York City is a city of "blocks"—the streets a grid of buildings. At night the city lights up with a crisp brilliance against the dark sky, add the quiet peace of a snowfall, stand at the top of the Empire State Building. It's like no other city in the world. OFFICER ROBERT KARL NYPD NYFD - Police Officer–16 years; Emergency Service Unit Truck 9 Elmont Fire Department–17 years; 1st Lieutenant-Rescue Company Captain- EMS Squad Firefighter- Engine Co #3. Officer Karl survived 9/11/01 at the WTC. Fourteen members of NYPD Emergency Services are still missing.

HOME OF THE BRAVE

30" x 36" Andrea Blackhurst
Wright-Patterson Air Force Base, OH USA

My quilt is a memorial to the men and women of the Pentagon whose lives were lost on September 11, 2001, and a tribute to those that serve our country everyday. I was personally affected as my husband recently finished a five-year assignment at the Pentagon and was scheduled to be there the next day. I was inspired by the phone calls I received that morning from concerned family and friends. The relief I felt soon turned to grief for the many military and civilian families that suffered the ultimate loss.

BITS OF RED, WHITE, AND BLUE

28" x 28" Sandra Kosch
Shelby, NE USA

The events of September 11th have forever changed our lives and our future. To honor the victims of the September 11th Terror Attack, I have sewn bits of red, white, and blue, the colors of the American Flag into a wreath…The thirteen shining stars stand for the original thirteen colonies. After 200 years, the beliefs and ideals of our forefathers that helped form this nation are still held high. That is part of what makes American the country it is today. The shape of the United States of America represents our nation…United as never before… This unbelievable act of terror has sent ripples throughout our country as well as the world. September 11th will be a day remembered forever.

The wreath was a published pattern in Quiltmaker, No. 74-76 by Cindy Wilson of Montello, Wisconsin

FIREBALL

11¼" x 11¾" Jaye A.H. Lapachet
Daly City, CA USA

I purchased most of these fabrics over Labor Day weekend thinking that I might use them together sometime. After September 11, 2001, I decided that I wanted to make a small woven quilt and that these fabrics would work together very well for the piece. I didn't realize until all the strips were woven together that this quilt looked like a fireball or explosion. I cannot make sense of these terrorist actions in my own mind much less explain it to my child or anyone else. This quilt shows part of what our country is experiencing: chaos. The fact that the fabrics are unified also show that our country has come together and become more unified after a long period of people being very separate from each other and not thinking about anyone, but themselves. Kiss your loved ones every day and say something kind to someone you don't know.

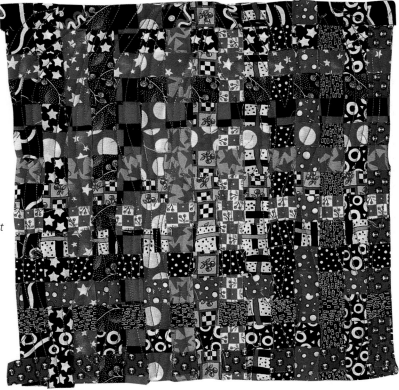

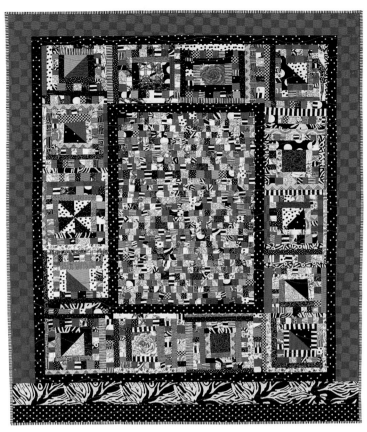

911 SKYSCRAPER

40" x 47" Karen Griska
Franklin, TN USA

This skyscraper/tombstone, made up of pieces of wreckage, evolved as I listened to the awful news of the terrorist attack.

I was shocked and sad. I prayed that God would be right there to hold the victims in His arms, help the rescue workers, comfort the worried and brokenhearted, give wisdom and courage to our President and his advisors, and to thwart any further terrorist schemes. I was shaken to realize that all this was happening Right now; and I kept listening and sewing, finishing this quilt five days later.

I have been very glad to see the outpouring of love and patriotism across this country. The roses in my quilt represent this love. I hope my quilt touches you.

FANS OF FREEDOM, FRIENDSHIP, AND FAITH

14½" x 14½" Mary Frances Wasson
Needville, TX USA

With assistance from Nanette Gaskey, Richardson, Texas. Nanette and I worked on this mini-wallhang-ing together in memory of the tragic events of September 11, 2001 in New York, Pennsylvania, and Washington D.C. Each of the fans symbolize the freedom, friendship, and faith that makes this a great country.

STARS AND STRIPES FOREVER

80" x 100" River City Quilters' Guild

Sacramento, CA USA

This quilt was a group effort from our community Outreach committee of the River City Quilters' Guild. The quilt was made by; Charla Ward, Jill Schroeder, John Brown, Sue Glass, Jeanne Auslam, and Patrice Stafford. It was started before the attacks on the World Trade Center and Pentagon on 9/11. It was finished quickly as a result of the tragic events, to express our patriotism and our love for the red, white, and blue of Old Glory...may the Stars and Stripes wave forever.

PEACE TO OUR AMERICAN PATRIOTS

61" x 49" Lisa Donigian

Beavercreek, OH USA

As a military wife, the moment I watched the second tower strike on September 11th, I knew that my husband would be called into action to defend our nation.

I designed this quilt to remember the heroes of September 11th. Every person who perished on that day is a true hero. In particular, I commend the firefighters, police, and medical personnel in New York and the brave men who took down the flight over Pennsylvania. The symbols on the quilt commemorate the date...9/11/01. There are nine peace doves, eleven stars and one proud American flag. Peace to all our American patriots... we will miss each of you and never forget your sacrifice.

CHRISTMAS IN RED, WHITE, AND BLUE

64" x 64" Arlene Alford

Batavia, OH USA

The evergreen symbolizes God's Promise that this too shall pass. Let us pray for those with a vacant seat at their holiday gathering. Let us realize how fortunate we are to be able to hold our family and friends even closer. Let us remember: "But I am sure I have always thought of Christmas time, when it has come round...as a good time. A kind, forgiving, charitable, pleasant time. The only time I know of ...when men and women seem by one consent to open their shut-up hearts freely, and to think of people as if they really were fellow-passengers to the grave, and, not another race of creatures bound on other journeys."
—Charles Dickens, A Christmas Carol

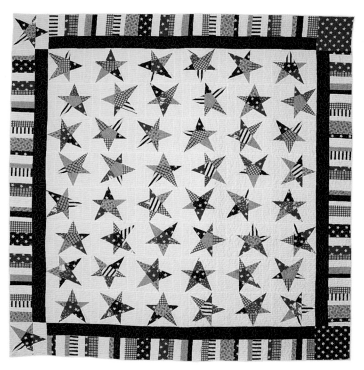

STARS AND STRIPES FOREVER

74" x 79" Audrey W. Christman
Washington, PA USA

This quilt is in remembrance of the good times I had over 50 years ago growing up on City Island, Bronx, NYC. There was a small park that we played in and a cubicle that the N.Y.P.D. used as a base. They sure treated us with good spirit...On Schofield Street was the N.Y.F.D. firehouse and they also were great to a bunch of pesky kids. I feel that the education and many skills I learned in NYC have helped me all these years. We moved from NYC forty-one years ago. After September 11th, my mind went back to the many friends I have and the good times we shared.

This quilt has fifty stars representing all the states in this great country. It also represents the harmony and unity this tragedy has brought us. The bright colors represent our prayers for a brighter future.

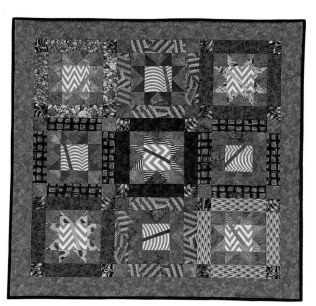

WORLD TRADE CENTER I

42" x 42" Debby Timby
Portsmouth, RI USA

During the days after the attack on the World Trade Center and the Pentagon, I was riveted to the TV, filled with horror and unfocused energy. One of the images particularly astonished me—that of the grayness and lack of color after the World Trade Center buildings collapsed, except for the tiny flashes of color of the rescue workers' hardhats and the seemingly tiny heavy equipment. This quilt is my attempt to interpret that, but it also has various fabrics that evoke people falling, the hands of rescue workers, mangled building pieces, rubble, burning buildings and the American flag...

AMERICAN PLANES IN THE SKY

40" x 40" Karen Antis
Evansville, IN USA

I chose to call my quilt American Planes in the Sky. With the patriotic fabrics and the Flying Geese pattern, it just seemed appropriate. I was so overwhelmed by 9/11 ...Sewing was the only thing that kept my sanity intact. I hope we get the job done that we are over there to do.

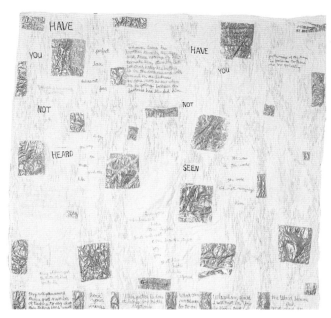

Blinded by the Darkness

48" x 44" Kimberly Baxter-Packwood
Ames, IA USA

Life is both precious and precarious. The only thing I thought about, when I saw these buildings being destroyed, was these people are so blinded by their own hatred that they stand in total darkness.

When I decided to make the quilt I knew it would be white, and struggled with what white had to do with darkness, as I prayed and meditated over the scriptures I wanted to use, I begun to realized that the darkness doesn't like to be exposed. The light can be stark raw place that requires love and honestly. Hate does not exist in the light. I am commanded to love my God, my brothers, and my enemies without exception, to do otherwise would mean living in darkness, without God.

Sweet Land of Liberty

26" x 26" Miri Cook
Moshavat Migdal, Israel

The terrorist attack of September 11th was so shocking that it is still difficult to wrap my mind around it, and comprehend what I saw with my eyes. Living in Israel, where we have suffered from terrorist attacks for decades…This quilt…expresses my feelings that light shines from liberty and will continue to shine. Terror is as much a psychological attack as a physical one but Americans have already shown their resilience and strength, gained from their commitment to the values that make America the Land of the Free.

Missing Man Formation

42" x 42" Elizabeth Gonzalez
Ketchikan, Alaska USA

As we reflect on the events of September 11, 2001 we mourn for the incredible loss of life, we rejoice for the renewed spirit of patriotism for the Great Country we live in, we pray for the men and women of our military who will be defending our freedoms.

The missing man formation is a military tradition, which honors fallen flyers, by flying a formation with one plane missing.

This quilt is to honor the thousands of lives lost through the senseless acts of September 11th…

FROM DARKNESS INTO THE LIGHT

26" x 36" Sydney Stilling
Missouri City, TX USA

God is our refuge and strength, an ever-present help in trouble. Therefore we will not fear, though the earth give way, and the mountains fall.—Psalm 46: 1-2

This quilt represents my belief that while Evil may have destroyed the bodies of thousands of people on September 11, 2001, it had no power over the souls of those who believed in God. Those souls now rest in God's hands.

The "rubble" at the base of the buildings is filled with items that are reminders of those lost on that day…The "windows" in the buildings are reflecting the flames from the rubble. The dove represents the souls of those who believed in Him soaring up into God's hands. May they rest in peace.

This quilt is dedicated to those brave and selfless firefighters and policemen who performed their duties with grace, honor, and courage. While most people were fleeing for their lives, they were going into the burning buildings to help those in need. It is also dedicated to those members of United Airlines Flight 93, who sacrificed their lives, so that others would not be killed.

This will be the exhibit I remember forever.

REBIRTH: FROM FIRE AND ASHES

18" x 38" Mary Jo Hodge
Eden, NY USA

Like the phoenix of old reborn from the fire, from fire and from ashes, our eagle soars high. We lift up our hearts to salute our bold heroes, the spirit of freedom lives anew from Ground Zero.

AFTER

14" x 17" Patricia Klem
Rancho Santa Fe, CA USA

I believe that God must be looking into the hearts of His children and shedding tears at the way we are treating one another —especially in His name. It is my prayer that after these misguided actions of September 11, 2001, people of all religions will come together in the understanding that we are all children of God. May His tears nourish our growth and compassion. The flowers have the symbols of the world's five major religions: Christianity, Islam, Judaism, Buddhism, and Hinduism.

HALF MAST AT ANCHOR

11¼" x 14¼" Carolyn Lee Vehslage
Erial, NJ USA

On September 8, 2001 we left Long Beach Island, New Jersey aboard our thirty-six foot Mariner Yacht, Fandango for our annual two-week sailboat cruise. We were going to circum-navigate Long Island, NY and pass right by the Towers along the East River of Manhattan on our way back to our homeport. We were anchored in Montauk harbor at the north tip of Long Island when we learned of the tragic events. For the duration of our cruise, we flew our yacht ensign at half-mast. It is the nautical version of the American flag and has an anchor surrounded by a circle of thirteen stars. This quilted wall hanging is our tribute to all the souls lost on September 11, 2001.

WHISPERS AMID THE DUST

18" x 13½" Shelia Baird
Aberlady, East Lothian Scotland, UK

As I watched the tragedies in America unfolding on television, my first reactions were horror, disbelief and sadness. A few days later I saw this poem sent to our local newspaper. It gave me the inspiration to make this simple wallhanging in memory of all who were killed on the September 11th. And with the hope that those of us who remain will find the strength and resolve to bring about a better world where all people can live in peace and harmony.

WISHES FOR THE WORLD

87" x 88" Betsy Shannon
Minneapolis, MN USA

In the spring of 2000, I made this quilt to convey my feelings about the world I believe in. My inspiration was the place of my employment, a church in the poor, rough neighborhood of Minneapolis, where people of many faiths, including the faithless work together towards a unified goal...My message, seemingly profound, is simple. Every person on this earth deserves a place to live, food to eat and education, a loving family and an accepting and welcoming community.

As these basics are met, all would share in the gift of each other's uniqueness and all would join together in the care and respect of our planet. Then there would be no space or time for hatred.

These wishes for the world, I pray.

TEARS: A HEALING QUILT

46" x 68" Judy B. Dales
Kingwood, TX USA

This quilt was not made in response to the events of September 11th, but because it speaks of grief, it is appropriate for this exhibit.

I made Tears in 1991 to help me deal with my mother's death...At the time, I felt this was not surprising because I had spent so much time crying and grieving for my mother.

After the quilt was finished, I chose the title because I came to realize that tears are a normal, healthy part of the grieving process and can be enormously comforting.

Immediately after the events of September 11th, most of us were too numb and shocked to cry. As time passed, however, I found myself crying at the oddest moments, and realized that, once again, tears were helping me deal with a difficult experience. We, as individuals, and as a nation, must not be shamed by our tears, but let them flow freely...

LIBERTY ENDURES

50" x 30" Ann M. Flaherty
Sanford, NC USA

When I first experienced the photograph that inspired this quilt—Lady Liberty against New York City's new smoky, somber skyline—the devastation seemed overwhelming. The solid presence of Lady Liberty, with her flame of Freedom—our national symbol for all that is good in our United States of America—shone through my despair.

I am so proud of the emergency service, fire department, police, and port authority personnel; the soldiers; and ordinary citizens whose innate acts of heroism on September 11, 2001 saved so many more lives. America's response with blood, money, volunteerism, and a faith that is stronger than we've ever experienced in our lifetimes showed the world that, thick or thin, we stand together.

The knowledge that Liberty will endure all comforts me. As my dear friends, neighbors, and family members are sent to battle the evil that has invaded our collective psyche, I have confidence that they will...that America will...prevail.

Thank you Associated Press and photographer Dan Loh for capturing the image that inspired me to create this quilt.

Index of Quilt Makers